OCCASIONAL PAPER 240

Debt-Related Vulnerabilities and Financial Crises

An Application of the Balance Sheet Approach to Emerging Market Countries

Christoph Rosenberg, Ioannis Halikias, Brett House, Christian Keller, Jens Nystedt, Alexander Pitt, and Brad Setser

D1529994

INTERNATIONAL MONETARY FUND
Washington DC
2005

© 2005 International Monetary Fund

Production: IMF Multimedia Services Division
Typesetting: Alicia Etchebarne-Bourdin

Cataloging-in-Publication Data

Debt-related vulnerabilities and financial crises: an application of the balance
   sheet approach to emerging market countries/Christoph Rosenberg . . .
   [et al.]—Washington, D.C.: International Monetary Fund, 2005.

         p.   cm.—(Occasional paper; no. 240)

Includes bibliographical references.
ISBN 1-58906-425-9

   1. Financial statements—Developing countries. 2. Financial statements—
Developing countries—Statistics. 3. Financial crises—Developing countries.
I. Rosenberg, Christoph B. II. Occasional paper (International Monetary Fund);
no. 240.
HF5681.B2D32 2005

Price: US$25.00
(US$22.00 to full-time faculty members and
students at universities and colleges)

Please send orders to:
International Monetary Fund, Publication Services
700 19th Street, N.W., Washington, DC 20431, U.S.A.
Tel.: (202) 623-7430   Telefax: (202) 623-7201
E-mail: publications@imf.org
Internet: http://www.imf.org

recycled paper

Contents

Figures

Tables

The following symbols have been used throughout this paper:

. . . to indicate that data are not available;

— to indicate that the figure is zero or less than half the final digit shown, or that the item does not exist;

– between years or months (e.g., 2003–04 or January–June) to indicate the years or months covered, including the beginning and ending years or months;

/ between years (e.g., 2003/04) to indicate a fiscal (financial) year.

"n.a." means not applicable.

"Billion" means a thousand million.

Minor discrepancies between constituent figures and totals are due to rounding.

The term "country," as used in this paper, does not in all cases refer to a territorial entity that is a state as understood by international law and practice; the term also covers some territorial entities that are not states, but for which statistical data are maintained and provided internationally on a separate and independent basis.

Preface

The analysis of currency and maturity mismatches in sectoral balance sheets is increasingly becoming a regular element in the IMF's toolkit for surveillance in emerging market countries. This paper describes this so-called balance sheet approach and shows how it can be applied to detect vulnerabilities and shape policy advice. It also provides a broad-brush overview of how balance sheet vulnerabilities have evolved over the past decade and presents a number of case studies.

This study is derived from several papers prepared for the IMF's Executive Board, starting with "The Balance Sheet Approach to Financial Crisis" (IMF Working Paper No. 02/210). The project was initiated by Mark Allen, Director of the IMF's Policy Development and Review Department, who—along with Juha Kähkönen—provided general direction. The team that drafted this and the previous paper was led by Christoph Rosenberg and included Ioannis Halikias, Brett House, Christian Keller, Jens Nystedt, Alexander Pitt, and Brad Setser. At various stages, the project has benefited from comments by the IMF's Executive Board, management, various departments, and participants in several seminars organized by the European Central Bank, the Bank of England, the Bank of Canada, the IMF Institute, the Asia and Pacific Department, and the Policy Development and Review Department. In particular, the authors would like to acknowledge the contributions of Nouriel Roubini (who coauthored the earlier working paper), as well as Matthew Fisher, Olivier Jeanne, Leslie Lipschitz, Christian Mulder, Alan MacArthur, and Jeromin Zettelmeyer. Invaluable research assistance was provided by Rich Kelly and Gely Economopoulos. Esha Ray of the External Relations Department edited the paper and coordinated the production and publication.

The opinions expressed in the paper are those of the authors, and do not necessarily reflect the views of country authorities, the IMF, or IMF Executive Directors.

I Overview

This occasional paper describes the conceptual framework of the so-called balance sheet approach (BSA) and its application to emerging market countries. This type of analysis is increasingly used in the IMF's analysis of debt-related vulnerabilities, as evidenced by a growing number of Article IV consultation reports providing applications to individual countries. There is also a large body of academic literature that examines financial crises and their origins by using the BSA (Box 1.1). Moreover, the approach has become a standard element in the toolkit of risk assessments conducted by the private sector.

The paper has four related purposes:

- First, it introduces, in general terms, the BSA and its application to emerging market economies. Specifically, the paper seeks to explain some basic concepts underlying the approach and how they have been used to examine the origins and consequences of recent financial crises.

- Second, it provides an overview of salient balance sheet developments in emerging market economies. The paper takes account of the main balance sheet trends over the past decade and includes a number of case studies. Data weaknesses notwithstanding, the paper illustrates how intersectoral linkages have deepened over time. This suggests that the BSA is becoming increasingly relevant for vulnerability analysis.

- Third, it demonstrates how the BSA can be used to identify vulnerabilities. The paper should be seen mainly as a didactic device: both the broader regional overview as well as the country case studies illustrate how the BSA can be applied, even with relatively limited data. The paper also highlights the importance of systematically taking into account the level and structure of liabilities and assets in addition to traditional macroeconomic indicators. This facilitates analysis of the main linkages between domestic sectors, and consideration of off-balance-sheet activities, including contingent liabilities.

- Finally, it prepares the ground for discussing surveillance and program-related policy issues.

The paper seeks to provide empirical backing for the IMF Executive Board's recent conclusions regarding policies that can make emerging market economies more resilient, including appropriate liquidity management. For the design of IMF-supported programs, the paper provides some background for discussing how best to design debt-related conditionality, and how to justify access to IMF resources.

The paper focuses on emerging market countries, because this is where the application of the BSA appears particularly promising. First, several of these countries have been subject to capital account crises in the last decade, often emanating from balance-sheet-related weaknesses. They have proven particularly vulnerable to sudden capital outflows and sharp changes in investors' confidence, interest rates, and exchange rates because their financing is generally less diversified than in mature countries: they are typically not able to issue foreign debt in domestic currency and are often forced to borrow at short maturities. This may lead to combined currency and maturity mismatches. Moreover, there are fewer avenues to hedge or absorb financial losses.[1] Second, unlike in industrial countries where balance sheet analysis is already widely used and the related risks are factored into policy formulation, IMF staff's work on emerging market countries has more potential to provide new insights and identify avenues for research. Finally, the IMF's current budget constraints dictate a risk-oriented approach where IMF staff resources are concentrated on members that are most likely to be subject to crisis and where the IMF could be—or is already—financially exposed.

The BSA as a conceptual framework is, of course, relevant for mature markets as well. In fact, balance sheet issues feature prominently in the IMF's surveillance of industrial countries. For example, re-

---

[1]Recent empirical work has established that the types of crises for which balance sheet mismatches have strong predictive power, notably "sudden stops," have tended to be an exclusive feature of emerging market economies. See, for example, Calvo, Izquierdo, and Mejía (2004).

Box 1.1. The Balance Sheet Approach in the Academic Literature

Until the mid-1990s, the standard "first generation" model explained currency crises usually as the result of monetized fiscal deficits that would lead to reserve losses and eventually the abandonment of an exchange rate peg. The emphasis was on fundamental macroeconomic factors and the idea that a crisis would be triggered more or less mechanically, once reserves had fallen to a critical level (Krugman, 1979; Flood and Garber, 1984).

The "second generation" crisis models developed after the European exchange rate mechanism crisis in 1992 and the Mexican crisis in 1994–95 can be seen as the first formal recognition of the potential role of balance sheet mismatches in currency crises. In these models, crisis can be triggered by an endogenous policy response as the authorities decide whether to devalue based on trade-offs, for example, between the benefits of a strong currency and the costs of higher unemployment.[1] In addition to fundamental weaknesses (such as an overvalued currency and an unsustainable current account deficit), they point out how maturity and currency mismatches may lead to a self-fulfilling currency run, a debt rollover crisis, or a bank run (multiple equilibria).

Following the experience of the Asian crisis of 1997–98, where private sector vulnerabilities rather than fiscal imbalances played a key role, a "third generation" of models has been explicitly based on balance sheet analysis. While crises were seen to have some elements of a self-fulfilling "liquidity run" (see Sachs and Radelet, 1998; Rodrik and Velasco, 1999), these models brought to the open a number of additional vulnerabilities in the corporate and financial

sector, and also highlighted that currency crises are often followed by banking crises ("twin crises"). A wide range of models based on balance sheet analysis were developed to understand how capital account movements drive currency and financial crises (see Dornbusch, 2001).

Different strands of these third generation models emphasize diverse factors, including microeconomic distortions, currency mismatches, self-fulfilling runs, or capital reversals. Work by Krugman (1999), Masson (1999), and Corsetti, Pesenti, and Roubini (1999a and 1999b) points to weakly supervised and regulated financial systems, directed lending, moral hazard caused by government guarantees, and distortions created by fixed exchange rates. Another body of work stresses how large currency depreciation in the presence of foreign currency liabilities increases the real debt-service burden, leading to investment and output contraction.[2] The initial currency depreciation is triggered by fundamental shocks, but in some models it is a self-fulfilling process, where an expected depreciation leads to a currency run and a collapse of the peg, and the resulting real depreciation wipes out the private sector's balance sheets, thus ex post validating the confidence loss and the currency crash. Indeed, Chang and Velasco (1999), Burnside, Eichenbaum, and Rebelo (1998), and Schneider and Tornell (2000) interpret financial crises as international variants of "bank run" models (as in Diamond and Dybvig, 1983). Recent work in the IMF's Research Department shows how the self-fulfilling run caused by the feedbacks between the currency depreciation and balance sheet deterioration can

[1]See Obstfeld (1994); Drazen and Masson (1994); and Cole and Kehoe (1996).

[2]See Krugman (1999); Céspedes, Chang, and Velasco (2000); Gertler, Gilchrist, and Natalucci (2003); Aghion, Bachetta, and Banerjee (2000); and Cavallo, Kisselev, Perri, and Roubini (2002).

cent Article IV consultations for Australia, Ireland, the United Kingdom, and the United States focused on potential changes in real estate values and the implications for mortgage lending and household debt. The international linkages of the banking and insurance sectors have been the subject of selected issues papers for Germany, Portugal, and Spain. In the case of Austria, currency mismatches (rapidly expanding

foreign currency loans to households) have been the subject of staff scrutiny. These studies have all looked into specific sectors, and data provided by the authorities have generally been adequate. A full-fledged intersectoral balance sheet analysis is very data intensive, but some industrial country members (such as the United Kingdom) are trying to make progress in this area.

be avoided through an international lender of last resort (Jeanne and Wyplosz, 2001; Zettelmeyer and Jeanne, 2002).

The recent literature on debt intolerance emphasizes that developing countries historically have run into problems at much lower debt-to-output ratios than advanced countries.[3] This research focuses on weak revenue bases and the lack of expenditure control as critical reasons in explaining why primary balances and hence sustainable public debt levels in an emerging market economy are fairly low.[4] In the context of balance sheet analysis, these traditional indicators of fiscal weaknesses can be interpreted as vulnerabilities on the asset side of the public sector's balance sheet. Other research highlights the role weaknesses on the liability side of the public sector's balance sheet can play in reducing the level of debt that emerging market economies can sustain. For example, the literature on original sin—the inability to borrow (abroad, but also at home) long term in the local currency—draws attention to important differences between the debt structures of advanced economies and many emerging market economies.[5]

Financial crises, especially in Latin America, have inspired additional research on the vulnerabilities associated with (partial) domestic dollarization in emerging market countries.[6] Households' holdings of dollar deposits, for example, can leave the banking system and the overall economy vulnerable to a self-reinforcing deposit run as a shock to the portfolio preferences of domestic households prompts a shift out of domestic dollar deposits toward relatively safer international assets. The need to match dollar deposits with domestic dollar loans can increase the overall stock of foreign-currency-denominated claims in the economy, aggravating the risk that a currency depreciation will result in financial distress.[7] Balance sheet mismatches in the financial, household, or corporate sectors can seriously limit the degree of exchange rate volatility that policymakers are willing to tolerate (fear of floating) as monetary authorities in practice often intervene to prevent large movements in the exchange rate.[8] Recent work on currency mismatches by Goldstein and Turner (2004) highlights the need to take into account domestic foreign currency liabilities as well as external debt in assessing vulnerability, and to assess an economy's foreign currency debt in light of both existing stocks of foreign assets and its ability to generate a flow of foreign currency receipts from exports and income.

---

[3]Reinhart, Rogoff, and Savastano (2003a) find that *external* debt was less than 60 percent of GNP in 47 percent of the default cases they examined. Similarly, International Monetary Fund (2002b) and Manasse, Roubini, and Schimmelpfennig (2003) estimate external debt thresholds of 40 percent of GDP and 50 percent of GDP, respectively, beyond which countries are more likely to experience debt defaults.

[4]Research in International Monetary Fund (2003a) suggests that, based on fiscal performance, the sustainable gross public debt level for a typical emerging market economy may only be about 25 percent of GDP; 50 percent of GDP is found to be a threshold level beyond which the risk of a sovereign debt crisis increases significantly.

[5]Eichengreen, Hausmann, and Panizza (2003).

[6]Reinhart, Rogoff, and Savastano (2003b); De Nicoló, Honohan, and Ize (2003); Caballero and Krishnamurthy (2000); Baliño, Bennett, and Borensztein (1999); Mongardini and Mueller (2000); Oomes (2003); Edwards (2001); Havrylyshyn and Beddies (2003).

[7]Zettelmeyer and Jeanne (2002); Kaminsky and Reinhart (1999); and Jeanne and Wyplosz (2001).

[8]Calvo and Reinhart (2000); Céspedes, Chang, and Velasco (2000).

This paper is structured as follows: Section II introduces some general concepts underlying the BSA and shows how they can help better understand modern-day financial crises. Section III takes a broad look at trends in public and private balance sheets in emerging market countries, highlights their increasing linkages, and points to the vulnerabilities that they may create. Section IV aims to give a better sense of how such vulnerabilities can actually translate into real crises by more closely tracing balance sheet developments, both in a few recent crisis cases (Argentina, Turkey, and Uruguay) and in some near-crisis cases (Brazil, Lebanon, and Peru). Section V provides some concluding thoughts on policy implications, operationalizing the BSA, and further work.

II Balance Sheet Shocks and Their Transmission in Capital Account Crises

There is a growing recognition that the traditional financial programming approach may not fully explain some of the dynamics underlying modern-day capital account crises. Its flow-based analysis focuses on the gradual buildup of unsustainable fiscal and current account positions. The BSA, by contrast, focuses on shocks to stocks of assets and liabilities that can trigger large adjustments in (capital) flows. Such an approach can, therefore, be a useful complement to traditional flow analyses. Indeed, academics and policymakers have been paying increasing attention to the BSA's further development as a result of the capital account crises of the 1990s. The IMF has been applying the insights from the BSA for some time and many of its elements have entered the IMF's work on fiscal and external sustainability, liquidity and debt management, financial sector assessment, and so on.

Balance Sheet Concepts

An economy can be viewed as a stylized system of the balance sheets of all its agents. Unlike the more traditional analysis of an economy that looks at the *flows* occurring over a defined period of time—such as the annual output, fiscal balance, current account balance, or investment flows—a balance sheet analysis looks at *stocks* of assets and liabilities—such as debt, foreign reserves, loans outstanding, and inventory at a certain point in time. Obviously, the two approaches are interrelated, as the difference in a stock variable at two dates is related to the flow in the period between them.[2]

As a first step, one may identify an economy's main sectoral balance sheets: the government sector (including the central bank), the private financial sector (mainly banks), and the nonfinancial sector (corporations and households).[3] These sectors have claims on and liabilities to each other, and to external (nonresident) entities. When *consolidating* the sectoral balance sheets into the *country's* balance sheet, the assets and liabilities held between residents net out, leaving the country's external balance vis-à-vis the rest of the world (nonresidents).[4] Figure 2.1 shows a stylized system of such accounts, which excludes nonfinancial assets and liabilities. It illustrates how one sector's liability is by definition another sector's asset, and vice versa.

Sectoral balance sheets provide important information that remains hidden in the consolidated country balance sheet. A country's balance sheet can show the potential scale of vulnerability to reversals in external financing flows, but it is often inadequate for examining the genesis of such reversals. Weaknesses in certain sectoral balance sheets may contribute to the creation of a country-wide balance of payments crisis, yet they may not appear in a country's aggregate balance sheet. An important example is *foreign currency debt between residents*, which is netted out of a country's aggregated balance sheet. Nevertheless, if the government is unable to roll over its hard currency debts to residents and must draw on its reserves to honor its debts, such debts can trigger an external balance of payments crisis. The risk that

---

[2]The change in stock is a combination of changes in valuation of the existing stock of assets and liabilities, and net additions to the stock from flows during the preceding period.

[3]For the purposes of the following analysis, it is most important to distinguish assets that in the event of a crisis are under the control of the country authorities from those that are controlled by the private sector. To simplify the presentation, the separation of the government and the central bank is therefore not highlighted. The distinction between monetary and fiscal authorities—part of the internationally accepted statistical guidelines—is, of course, important for many other purposes, not least to reflect central bank independence and also the IMF's lending to a country's monetary as opposed to its fiscal authorities. In general, the statistical format used here can be adjusted to that of the System of National Accounts 1993—with flexibility in the sectorization of an economy and taking into account country circumstances.

[4]In official balance of payments statistics, the balance sheet of the stock of external financial assets and liabilities, broken down in four sectors, is referred to as the *international investment position* (see International Monetary Fund, 1993).

Figure 2.1. Sectoral Balance Sheets and Their Main Interlinkages

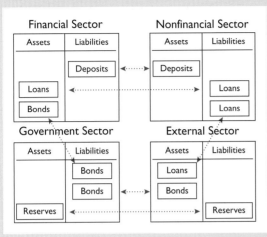

The Anatomy of Recent Balance Sheet Crises

Capital account crises typically occur as creditors suddenly lose confidence in the health of the balance sheets of one of a country's main sectors—the banking system, the corporate sector, or the government. This confidence loss can prompt sudden and large-scale portfolio adjustments, such as massive withdrawals of bank deposits, panic sales of securities, or abrupt halts of debt rollovers. As the exchange rate, interest rates, and other asset prices adjust, the balance sheets of an entire sector—which may be largely solvent in the absence of these adverse events—can sharply deteriorate. In an integrated financial system and with an open capital account, concerns about asset quality on domestic balance sheets can provoke creditors to shift toward (safer) foreign assets. This will often result in capital outflows, which exert further pressure on the exchange rate or official reserves and ultimately result in a balance of payments crisis. The mechanisms underlying such balance sheet crises, which are illustrated in Figure 2.2, are discussed in more detail below.

The initial shock to a balance sheet may take various forms, its impact depending on the existing mismatches on the balance sheet. Several patterns can be detected in capital account crises of the last decade:

difficulties rolling over domestic debts can spill over into a balance of payments crisis is particularly acute in a world where capital accounts have been liberalized. Such risks are enhanced if difficulties in one sector can cascade into healthy sectors as a result of financial interlinkages.

Four general types of risks are worth highlighting when assessing balance sheet weaknesses: maturity, currency, capital structure, and solvency. Maturity and currency mismatches create exposure to particular sources of risk, including market risks such as a change in interest rates or exchange rates, while capital structure mismatches reduce a country's ability to bear these as well as a range of other risks.[5] All of these mismatches create vulnerabilities that can lead directly to solvency risk, although solvency risk can also arise from other sources.[6] The interaction of these risks can be best understood when examining how they have come to bear in recent emerging market financial crises.

---

[5]Pettis (2001) and others whose analyses are grounded in corporate finance use the term "capital structure" to refer to the maturity and currency composition of an entity's debts, as well as the debt to equity ratio. Because maturity and currency risk are of particular importance for countries, this paper isolates these sources of risk. This paper uses the term capital structure only to refer to the balance between debt and equity, not to the currency and maturity composition of debt.

[6]This is not an exhaustive list of the risks to a balance sheet. Moreover, there are other possible ways of breaking down various types of balance sheet risks than those discussed in this paper: for example, one could identify rollover risks, market risks (which would include both currency and interest rate risk), credit risk, operational risk, and solvency risks. The categorization laid out here has the advantage of highlighting the underlying mismatches that create sources of vulnerability from a *debtor's* perspective.

Figure 2.2. Anatomy of a Balance Sheet Crisis

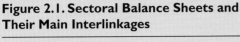

- A *currency mismatch*—a predominance of assets denominated in domestic currency over liabilities denominated in foreign currency—leaves a balance sheet vulnerable to a depreciation of the domestic currency (*exchange rate shock*).

- A *maturity mismatch*—long-term, illiquid assets mismatched against short-term liabilities expose a balance sheet to risks related both to rollover and to interest rates: if liquid assets do not cover maturing debts, a balance sheet is vulnerable to a *rollover risk*, because emerging market economies can find themselves shut out of capital markets altogether. Furthermore, a sharp increase in interest rates (*interest rate shock*) can dramatically increase the cost of rolling over short-term liabilities, leading to a rapid increase in debt service.

- Other *market risks* include any sharp drop in the price of assets such as government bonds, real estate, or equities, to which the balance sheets of a certain sector may be particularly exposed.

Any of the above shocks can bring about a deterioration in the value of a sector's assets compared with its liabilities and hence to a reduction of its net worth; in the extreme case this net worth may turn negative and the sector becomes insolvent. The greater a balance sheet's *capital structure mismatch*—too much debt relative to equity—the smaller its buffer against such an event.

Strong balance sheets protect against real as well as financial shocks. Many shocks originate in the real economy. For example, a collapse in the demand for a country's main commodity or other major export product will lead to a deterioration in corporate earnings or government revenue. This will prompt a reassessment of these sectors' sustainability and thus a reevaluation of the market value of their debt and other assets. Such real shocks are particularly dangerous when combined with financial vulnerabilities, as a real shock is often correlated with reduced market access. The impact of the commodity price shock of 1998, for example, was magnified in countries such as Russia, where maturity mismatches left balance sheets vulnerable to rollover risk and interest rate shocks.

Maturity and currency mismatches are sometimes hidden in indexed or floating rate debt instruments, making these mismatches less evident. In some emerging market economies (e.g., Brazil) liabilities may be formally denominated in local currency, but indexed to the exchange rate. Similarly, the nominal maturity of an asset may be long, but the interest rate it bears may be floating. Such indexation often creates the same mismatches as if the debt were denominated in foreign currency or as if the maturity were as short as the frequency of the interest rate adjustments.

Off-balance-sheet activities can substantially alter the overall risk exposure. Financial transactions such as forwards, futures, swaps, and other derivatives are not recorded on balance sheets, but imply predetermined or contingent future flows that will eventually affect them. Such transactions can be used to effectively reduce the risk created by balance sheet mismatches: for example, corporations with a foreign currency mismatch may enter into foreign currency forward contracts to reduce their exposure to exchange rate risk. By the same token, off-balance-sheet activities increase risk exposure when they are not used to hedge (taking a position that is negatively correlated to an existing balance sheet risk), but to speculate, or, in the particular case of monetary authorities, to support the domestic currency against market pressures.

Balance sheet problems in one sector can spill over into other sectors, often snowballing in the process. Balance sheet crises can originate in the corporate sector (as in some Asian countries in 1997–98) or the fiscal sector (as in Russia in 1998, Turkey in 2001, and, more recently, in some Latin American countries), with the banking sector playing a key transmission role in all these episodes. If a shock causes the corporate sector or the government to be unable to meet its liabilities, another sector, typically the banking sector, loses its claims. By the same token, if banks tighten their lending to prevent their asset portfolio from deteriorating, this further complicates the situation of a corporate sector or a government in dire need of fresh financing or a debt rollover. Because of these repercussions, balance sheet problems tend to snowball as they spill from one sector into another.

A loss of confidence in the banking system often not only triggers a run on deposits, but also a flight from the currency. The authorities may expand liquidity or lower interest rates to support the ailing banking system, while depositors may seek to protect their savings by switching into foreign currency assets. Both create pressure on the exchange rate. A depreciating exchange rate, however, further weakens the asset side of a banking sector that has a currency mismatch on its balance sheet. Thus, banking and currency crises may reinforce each other, creating the "twin crises" frequently observed in past cases.

Although a crisis may not originate in the government's balance sheet, it is likely to spread to it, partly as a result of contingent liabilities. For instance, the banking system's integrity is often explicitly or implicitly guaranteed by the government. In the event of a crisis, such contingent (off-balance-sheet) commitments become definite (balance sheet) liabilities, further adding to the deterioration of the government's balance sheet and the fiscal pressures that are created by the macroeconomic disruptions resulting from the crisis. Contingent commitments may even exist to bail out corporations, especially when governments are involved in their investment and borrowing decisions. Furthermore, monetary authorities may be engaged in forward contracts and other off-balance-sheet transactions, which can entail large contingent drains on their foreign currency assets.

The interaction between financial balance sheets also magnifies the negative impact of a shock on real output levels. Autonomous investment cuts by corporations to restore the financial health of their balance sheets are usually compounded by a forced reduction in credit from distressed banks and lower consumption by households that experience a negative wealth effect. All this may contribute to a sharp decline in aggregate demand.

Operationalizing the Balance Sheet Approach

The IMF has been using insights based on balance sheet concepts in its surveillance work for some time. While this approach can also provide insights on crisis management and the design of IMF-supported programs, much of its recent application in the IMF has focused on vulnerability analysis. There is, for example, increased emphasis on the adequacy of official reserves in relation to short-term debt, monetary aggregates, and other stock variables; a sharpened focus on dollarization risks; and enhanced efforts at promoting better public liability management. Other important work that uses balance-sheet-related concepts includes the IMF's framework for debt sustainability analysis (DSA) and the Financial Sector Assessment Program (FSAP). Over the past few years, a number of country teams have applied the BSA to support their policy advice in the context of the annual Article IV consultations. Recent examples include Bulgaria, Colombia, Latvia, Lebanon, Peru, Thailand, and Turkey.

Efforts to incorporate the BSA into the IMF's work have been supported by statistical and transparency initiatives. These have improved the availability of some key balance sheet stock data and the accuracy of these data. In particular, the requirements of the Special Data Dissemination Standard (SDDS) have improved the dissemination of data and metadata on public and external debt, international reserves and foreign currency liquidity, international investment positions, and analytical accounts of the banking sector.[7] The IMF's Coordinated Portfolio Investment Survey has improved the availability and comparability of statistics on countries' portfolio investment positions. An interagency task force chaired by the IMF has also developed a new guide on the measuring and monitoring

of external debt.[8] The IMF's *Government Finance Statistics Manual 2001* supports the balance sheet approach through a statistical framework that systematically links flows and stocks and introduces the concept of a government balance sheet.

A simple matrix presentation of sectoral asset and liability positions can serve as the basis for a sectoral balance sheet analysis. There is, of course, no single well-established way of presenting and analyzing sectoral balance sheet data, and, obviously, more complex ways of modeling are possible, for example, by explicitly incorporating measures of volatility. For an outline of some operational aspects of the balance sheet approach, see Box 2.1.

A number of caveats regarding the usefulness of the BSA for vulnerability analysis are in order. While the application of the approach in this paper holds much promise, it also suffers from a number of shortcomings that will have to be overcome over time:

- First, as distinct from early warning systems, the BSA cannot be easily reduced to a small set of indicators that quantify vulnerabilities in a manner that is readily amenable to cross-country comparisons. Rather, the approach is better thought of as a conceptual framework for a fuller assessment of vulnerabilities and related policy options, in conjunction with other relevant country-specific factors.

- Second, by definition, the BSA does not take into account off-balance-sheet transactions that have become increasingly important over time. As will be demonstrated in some of the country case studies, such transactions can be used to hedge balance sheet exposures, but have at times exacerbated them.

- Third, a full assessment of underlying risks needs to factor in the probability distribution of key relevant shocks. For instance, under a fixed exchange rate regime, a situation of significant misalignment would raise the level of concern relating to any vulnerabilities identified by the BSA and sharpen the urgency of needed policy interventions.

- Finally, a full assessment of sectoral balance sheets on welfare grounds needs to take explicitly into account the relevant trade-offs between reducing vulnerability (along the lines suggested by the BSA) and minimizing financial cost. Such an approach is clearly required, for instance, when evaluating financial system liquidity, currency and maturity composition of external debt, and optimal reserve accumulation.

---

[7]See also "Data Provision to the Fund for Surveillance Purposes" (International Monetary Fund, 2002a).

[8]See International Monetary Fund (2003b).

Box 2.1. The Balance Sheet Approach in Practice

The aim of the balance sheet approach (BSA) is to provide a comprehensive assessment of currency and maturity mismatches across different sectors of an economy. The composition and size of assets and liabilities of an economy's main sectors provide information about the economy's vulnerability to crisis and the channels by which one sector's strengths or weaknesses could be transmitted to other sectors.

The operational foundation of the BSA is a matrix (see below) summarizing the asset and liability positions of the main sectors of the economy. Ideally, the analysis starts with a compilation of the data needed to fill the cells of this matrix for the public (including public enterprises), private financial, and private nonfinancial sectors vis-à-vis each other as well as the rest of the world. Data for the first two sectors are often readily available, while data for the nonfinancial private sector are usually harder to obtain. Information on the international investment position or external data sources (such as the Bank for International Settlements or the Special Data Dissemination Standard) can help in compiling the external position and deriving (as a residual) some of the unknown data elsewhere in the matrix. Data limita-

tions notwithstanding, the insights from even a partial analysis can be useful. Where data availability permits, the BSA can be augmented by including off-balance-sheet items, such as contingent claims or derivatives. A higher degree of sectoral disaggregation and a breakdown by instrument could also be useful, where data permit. Further, linkages across economies could be examined to assess possible routes for contagion.

The data in the matrix can then be used to quantify sectoral mismatches in the short and the medium term. From a vulnerability viewpoint, the most important classes of assets and liabilities would be those denominated in foreign currency, and their position vis-à-vis the rest of the world. In a second stage, there is the possibility of conducting stress tests, for example, by simulating a change in market valuations of sectoral assets. One could also simulate a depreciation of the domestic currency. However, since the main point of the BSA is to highlight the coverage of foreign-currency-denominated liabilities by corresponding assets, the discrepancy between these two is already an indicator of the stress that an economy would be exposed to in the event of a depreciation.

Intersectoral Asset and Liability Position

Issuer of Liability (Debtor)	Holder of Liability (Creditor)			
	Public sector	Financial private sector	Nonfinancial private sector	Rest of the world

Public sector (including central bank)
    Monetary base
    Total other liabilities
        Short-term
            Domestic currency
            Foreign currency
        Medium- and long-term
            Domestic currency
            Foreign currency				

Financial private sector
    Total liabilities
        Short-term
            Domestic currency
            Foreign currency
        Medium- and long-term
            Domestic currency
            Foreign currency
        Equity				

Nonfinancial private sector
    Total liabilities
        Short-term
            Domestic currency
            Foreign currency
        Medium- and long-term
            Domestic currency
            Foreign currency
        Equity				

Rest of the world
    Total liabilities
        Currency and short-term
        Medium- and long-term
        Equity				

III   Public and Private Sector Balance Sheets in Emerging Market Countries: Recent Trends and Key Risks

This section shows how public, banking, and non-financial private sector balance sheets in emerging market countries have become more integrated over the past decade.[9] It also provides a toolkit for assessing vulnerabilities, even with limited data. To highlight common trends and differences between 1992 and 2002, a sample of 25 emerging market countries is considered.[10] The countries are grouped into four regions: Latin America; East Asia; Central and Eastern Europe; and Middle East, Africa, and Turkey.[11] It should be noted at the outset that the small sample size for each region and sometimes sketchy data (especially for 1992) do not allow for a complete picture of relevant strengths and vulnerabilities. The primary purpose of this section is therefore to show the usefulness of the methodology rather than provide an authoritative view of the state of emerging market countries' balance sheets.

The Public Sector's Balance Sheet

The Liability Side

Public debt levels generally have increased over the last decade (Figure 3.1). The average debt-to-

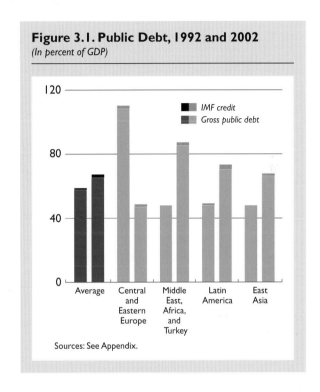

Figure 3.1. Public Debt, 1992 and 2002
(In percent of GDP)

Sources: See Appendix.

GDP ratio (including IMF credit) of emerging market economies has risen from 60 percent in 1992 to some 70 percent in 2002—levels generally viewed as cause for concern.[12] Europe is the only exception to the rising trend because some of these countries embarked on the transition process with very high debt ratios—partly attributed to the serious underestimation of GDP at the start of the period—which they subsequently managed to reduce.[13] The fiscal policy stance

---

[9]The public sector includes both the general government (in most countries including public enterprises) and the central bank.

[10]The sample consists of countries where public debt exceeds 30 percent of GDP, and where more than half of that debt is held by private creditors. This leaves out the universe of countries eligible for support under the Heavily Indebted Poor Countries Initiative or the International Development Association, but also some emerging market countries that have low public debt (e.g., the Czech Republic, the Baltic countries, and Chile) or a low share of privately held public debt (e.g., India). We also exclude small island economies such as the members of the Eastern Caribbean Currency Union, Jamaica, and Seychelles. For the exact regional country composition and detailed definitions of the variables and databases used, see the Appendix. The members covered in this sample account for 94 percent of all resources outstanding from the IMF's General Resources Account and 84 percent of total IMF resources outstanding. Owing to data limitations, data for years outside and within the range 1992–2002 are considered in some cases.

[11]Alternative groupings of the sample, such as by rating or capital market openness, were considered, but they ultimately did not provide for meaningful interpretation. Regional groupings, while imperfect, are stable over time, and have intuitive appeal.

---

[12]For a detailed analysis of public debt in emerging market countries see International Monetary Fund (2003a, Chapter III). In that country sample, emerging market countries in 2002 had an average public debt ratio of 70 percent, compared with 65 percent for industrial countries.

[13]This mainly reflects developments in Bulgaria and Poland, which brought down their debt ratios substantially (from 160 percent to 60 percent and from 80 percent to 50 percent, respectively) through, in part, debt restructurings and periods of high inflation.

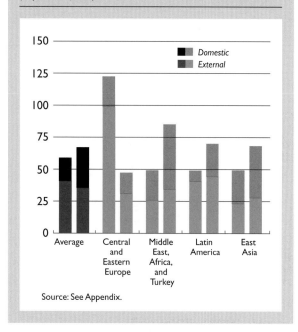

Figure 3.2. Public Domestic Versus Public External Debt, 1992 and 2002
(In percent of GDP)

Source: See Appendix.

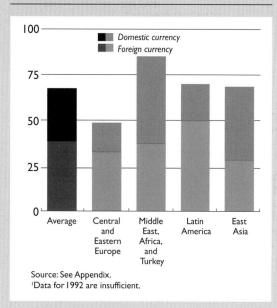

Figure 3.3. Public Domestic Versus Foreign Currency Debt, 2002[1]
(In percent of GDP)

Source: See Appendix.
[1]Data for 1992 are insufficient.

devaluations, have played a significant role in the rise of public (domestic) debt for the Asian crisis countries, but also for several in Latin America as well as Turkey.[14] The rise in public debt may be understated, as contingent liabilities arising, for example, from public guarantees in public-private partnerships—which have increased recently—are generally not recorded in the public debt statistics.

The share of domestically issued public debt has risen, outpacing the rise in external debt in most regions (Figure 3.2).[15] The growth of domestic debt markets reflects the success of many emerging market economies in reducing inflation and deepening financial markets, though, as noted above, in several cases, the placement of large domestic bond issues for bank recapitalization in the wake of financial crises contributed as well. As discussed below, domestic banks have often become significant holders of the sovereign's domestic debt, and, in some cases, of the sovereign's international debt as well, directly linking the soundness of the banking system to the sovereign's financial health.

There is little evidence that the risks associated with higher debt levels have been systematically offset by improved debt structures. In fact, at least in some regions, several measures point to an increased exposure to various market risks:

- *Currency risk.* Despite the growing importance of domestic debt, the share of foreign-currency-denominated debt is substantial (Figure 3.3). Many emerging market governments have difficulty placing long-term debt in their own currency on the domestic market. The critical mass needed to develop a sufficiently deep market may be missing, or investors may simply lack confidence in the stability of the domestic currency—an important factor in many of the Latin American and Middle Eastern countries where memories of high inflation are still fresh.[16] In this situation, governments have often resorted to indexing domestic debt to the exchange rate. Despite the debt's settlement in domestic cur-

---

[14]For example, Lindgren and others (1999, p. 65) estimate the total cost of bank restructuring in Indonesia after the 1997 crisis, including central bank liquidity support, the recapitalization of banks, and the purchase of nonperforming loans, at about 50 percent of GDP by mid-1999. The cost of recapitalizing domestic banking systems in Argentina, Brazil, Mexico, and Turkey on average added nearly 15 percent of GDP to the public sector debt ratio (Collyns and Kincaid, 2003, p. 7).

[15]Unless noted otherwise, in this paper "domestic" refers to debt issued under domestic governing law. Similarly, "international" or "external" refers to the debt's governing law rather than the residency of the creditor or the currency denomination of the debt.

[16]For a more detailed discussion, see Borensztein and others (2004).

is the underlying cause of the rise in public debt, but combined currency and banking crises, which involved large bank restructuring costs and currency

rency, this creates currency risk that is similar to debt denominated in foreign currency.[17]

- *Rollover risk.* Official holders of sovereign debt are being replaced by private holders (Figure 3.4)—a creditor group that is arguably less inclined to roll over its exposure at times of stress.[18] This trend also implies a shortening of maturities (Figure 3.5), as sovereign bonds issued on international capital markets tend to mature earlier (5–10 years) than debt owed to official creditors (15–30 years). Moreover, Brady bonds—often issued at (original) maturities of up to 30 years—have been increasingly swapped for regular global bonds with shorter maturities. However, the shortening of maturities also reflects a strategy to lower debt-service costs in the face of falling interest rates. While such aggregate measures say little about maturity structures (i.e., debt humps in particular years), they are indicative of a broad trend that debt contracts need to be renewed more frequently, exposing sovereigns to rollover risk.

- *Interest rate risk.* Comparable data for 1992 are not available, but in several countries—especially in Latin America—debt is linked to the local interest rate (floating debt), at times even to the central bank's overnight rate (Figure 3.6). Such debt may have a relatively extended maturity, implying reduced rollover risk. However, it carries many of the other risks associated with short-term debt. In particular, debt service becomes more onerous during economically difficult times when financial policies are often tightened.

As a result, emerging market public sector debt is quite sensitive to sudden swings in the exchange or interest rate. Standard stress tests from the IMF's DSA framework—a two-standard deviation shock to the short-term real interest rate and a 30 percent depreciation of the exchange rate—provide a rough sense of the vulnerabilities involved (Figure 3.7). The impact of the two shocks on emerging market public sector debt is substantial, in both cases raising the debt-to-GDP ratio by some 10 percentage points. A similar picture emerges if one examines the impact of a "joint" shock, which adds to these shocks a one-standard deviation decline of GDP growth and the primary fiscal balance.

[17]In the event of a devaluation, holders of foreign-exchange-linked debt may switch to foreign-exchange-denominated assets as they question the government's solvency. As the government services foreign-exchange-linked debt, it has to generate liquidity. In both cases, there will be pressures on reserves and/or the exchange rate. This type of debt is therefore included under foreign currency debt in Figure 3.3.

[18]There are exceptions to this general rule: in some countries (e.g., Israel and Lebanon) private investors can be as dedicated as official creditors.

Figure 3.4. Privately Held Versus Officially Held External Public Debt, 1992 and 2002
(In percent of total public debt)

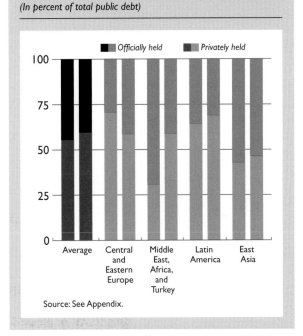

Source: See Appendix.

Figure 3.5. Average Maturity of Public External Debt, 1990–91 and 2000–01
(Stock of external public debt divided by two-year average of amortizations)

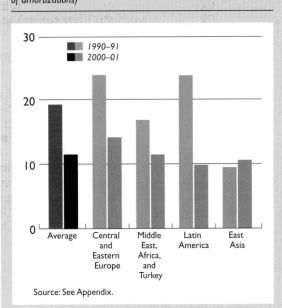

Source: See Appendix.

The Asset Side

The weakening of the liability side of the public sector's balance sheet has not, in general, been

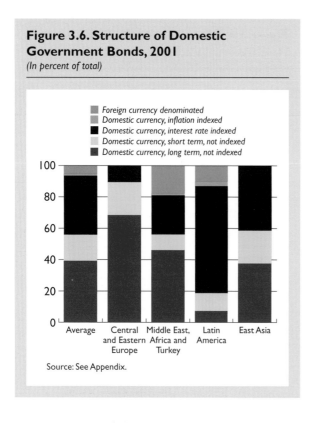

Figure 3.6. Structure of Domestic Government Bonds, 2001
(In percent of total)

- ◼ Foreign currency denominated
- ◼ Domestic currency, inflation indexed
- ◼ Domestic currency, interest rate indexed
- ◼ Domestic currency, short term, not indexed
- ◼ Domestic currency, long term, not indexed

Source: See Appendix.

matched by adequate improvements on the asset side. As discussed in International Monetary Fund (2003a), the lack of sufficient fiscal adjustment raises questions about emerging market countries' capacity to cope with the increase in public sector debt burdens.

- *Government primary surpluses.* Despite some improvement in revenue ratios, the sector's *net* assets (present values of flows) have generally worsened. Only in the European transition countries have average primary balances improved, but still remain negative (Figure 3.8).

- *Exports.* The ratio of public external debt to regular foreign currency inflows has generally improved (Figure 3.9). Taken at face value, this traditional measure of external viability may provide some comfort. But the flow of such receipts is not exclusively available to the public sector, as it increasingly competes with the needs of the private sector for foreign exchange.

The rise in official reserves is the main bright spot on the public sector's balance sheet over the past decade—although in some cases it mainly reflects large IMF credits. Reported holdings of the public sector's financial assets (both in dollar terms and as a share of GDP) are significantly higher across all

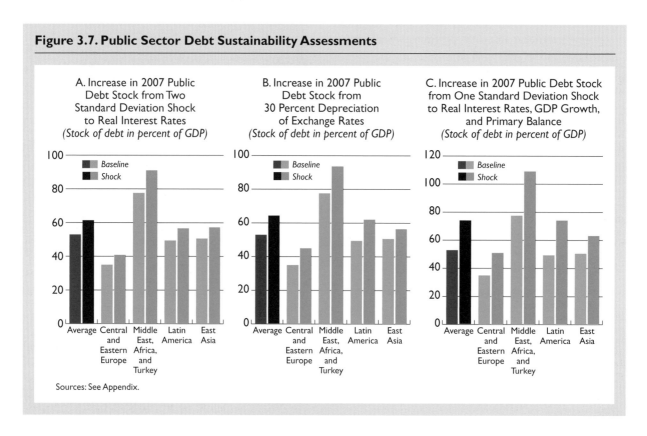

Figure 3.7. Public Sector Debt Sustainability Assessments

A. Increase in 2007 Public Debt Stock from Two Standard Deviation Shock to Real Interest Rates
(Stock of debt in percent of GDP)

B. Increase in 2007 Public Debt Stock from 30 Percent Depreciation of Exchange Rates
(Stock of debt in percent of GDP)

C. Increase in 2007 Public Debt Stock from One Standard Deviation Shock to Real Interest Rates, GDP Growth, and Primary Balance
(Stock of debt in percent of GDP)

- ◼ Baseline
- ◼ Shock

Sources: See Appendix.

regions, and especially in Asia (Figure 3.10).[19] However, reserves as a percent of GDP grew much slower in the Middle East, Africa, and Turkey region (owing to Turkey) and even declined in Latin America (owing to Argentina, Brazil, and Uruguay) if credit from the IMF is netted out. While higher reserve assets are a strength from a balance sheet perspective, they involve costs.

However, official reserve figures typically do not account for contingent liabilities on the central bank's balance sheet. The case studies in Section IV show how the private sector often has claims on the public sector's reserve assets, either from direct liabilities (e.g., deposits at the central bank) or as a result of the implicit contingent claims created by the public sector's policy commitments (e.g., protection from systemic banking crisis or commitment to a fixed exchange regime). For example, in economies with dollarized banking systems, domestic banks may hold foreign exchange assets at the central bank to meet reserve requirements. Because these constitute liabilities to residents, they are sometimes not counted against reported net international reserve figures. Nevertheless, such domestic liabilities are often a drain on reserves in periods of stress.[20] An assessment of reserve adequacy against broad measures of potential demand for foreign currency liquidity would provide a fuller picture of vulnerabilities.

The Financial Sector's Balance Sheet

The financial sector has grown in almost all regions, making the health of its balance sheet central to any assessment of economies' overall resilience to shocks (Figure 3.11).[21] Commercial banks' balance sheets are at the core of the allocation and transmission of risk in any economy. Maturity transformation—taking in short-term deposits to ex-

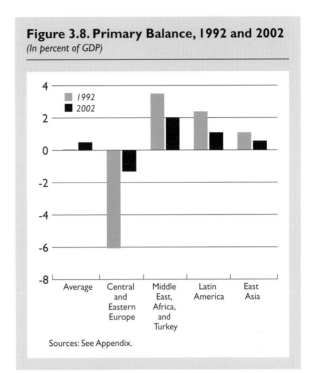

Figure 3.8. Primary Balance, 1992 and 2002
(In percent of GDP)

Sources: See Appendix.

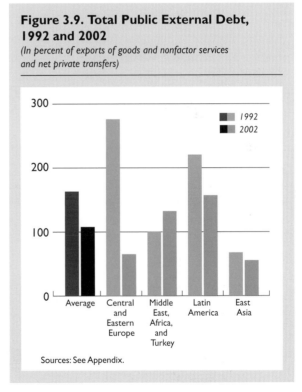

Figure 3.9. Total Public External Debt, 1992 and 2002
(In percent of exports of goods and nonfactor services and net private transfers)

Sources: See Appendix.

---

[19]In recent years some central banks have engaged in forward transactions, including so-called nondeliverable forwards, thereby creating contingent foreign currency claims that were not recorded on their published balance sheets. The IMF's "International Reserves and Foreign-Currency Liquidity: Guidelines for a Data Template" provides guidance on how to report such transactions in a transparent manner (see Kester, 2001).

[20]Some central banks use exchange-rate-linked money market instruments as part of their open market policy. For example, in a period of regional exchange rate pressures during the run up to the last Brazilian presidential elections, Peru's central bank experimented with issuing exchange-rate-linked certificates of deposit (CDs), in addition to the regular local currency CDs. Lebanon in 2003 issued high-yielding CDs denominated in domestic currency, but these could only be bought if an equivalent amount of foreign exchange was surrendered.

[21]For the purposes of this paper, due to data limitations, the financial sector is synonymous with the banking sector.

tend longer-term loans—is fundamental to financial intermediation, giving rise to the well-known risk of deposit runs. The financial systems of emerging market countries often face challenges not typically found in advanced economies: to accommodate

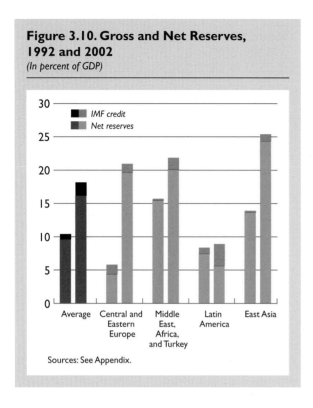

Figure 3.10. Gross and Net Reserves, 1992 and 2002

(In percent of GDP)

Sources: See Appendix.

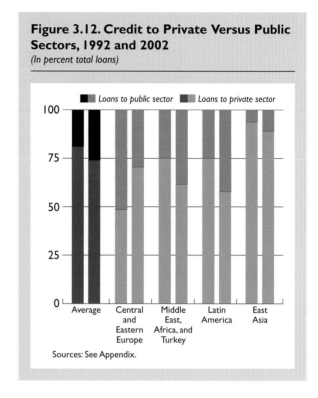

Figure 3.12. Credit to Private Versus Public Sectors, 1992 and 2002

(In percent total loans)

Sources: See Appendix.

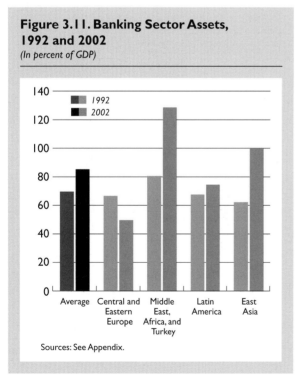

Figure 3.11. Banking Sector Assets, 1992 and 2002

(In percent of GDP)

Sources: See Appendix.

loan demand, banks may tap foreign credit lines; to attract depositors, banks may offer foreign currency deposits; banks may extend domestic loans in for-

eign currency to match their foreign currency liabilities; as a consequence of high public sector deficits, banks may have a large exposure to government paper. Also, supervisory frameworks and practices are often less developed than in advanced economies. On the other hand, the growth of the banking sector has in many countries been accompanied by a significant increase in foreign capital participation, which can lead to improved risk management practices. Parent banks are also a possible source of direct financial support at times of crisis. Further, in the wake of large financial crises, and aided by the FSAP, banking supervision has generally improved.

Banks' exposure to the sovereign generally has increased—a linkage that accentuates the potential for spillovers between the financial and the public sector (Figure 3.12). The increase in bank exposure to the public sector has been most pronounced in the Middle East and Latin America, with average public sector credit amounting to 40 percent of bank assets. Such interconnections between the balance sheets of the public sector and the banking system were particularly important during Argentina's 2001 crisis (see Section IV).

Bank balance sheets' direct and indirect exposure to currency risk has increased in the wake of an upsurge in foreign currency deposits and loans. Dollarization is another example of how domestic balance sheets interconnect:

- On average, 40 percent to 45 percent of bank deposits in Europe, Latin America, and the Middle East are denominated in foreign currency. In East Asia the share of foreign currency deposits remains much smaller, although the 2002 share of around 12 percent is twice that in 1992 (Figure 3.13). Patterns of such dollarization are highly uneven: in some countries (e.g., Croatia, Lebanon, and Uruguay) foreign currency deposits greatly exceed domestic currency deposits, while in others (e.g., Brazil) their share is zero because banking legislation does not permit the holding of foreign currency deposits. In the event of a devaluation, the liability side of banks' balance sheets would be greatly inflated.

- In an effort to balance their domestic foreign currency liabilities, banks have increased their foreign currency lending to residents (Figure 3.14). Thus, most domestic foreign currency deposits are offset by domestic foreign currency loans, not by assets held abroad (the banking sector's net foreign asset positions are positive, but close to balance). This implies that, in the event of an exchange rate adjustment, banks' balance sheets crucially depend on the performance of their domestic foreign currency loans and, ultimately, the existence of a viable export sector. Consequently, the exposure of the banking sector's balance sheet to currency risk cannot be adequately assessed without understanding currency mismatches on the balance sheets of the nonfinancial private sector.

Dollarization also implies that the banking system can be the source of large foreign currency liquidity needs in a crisis. Banks that undertake maturity transformation in foreign currency—offsetting short-term funding from domestic dollar deposits with less liquid domestic dollar-denominated loans—are vulnerable both to a run and to the risk that exchange rate fluctuations will lead to a sharp deterioration in the quality of a bank's loan portfolio (credit risk). As the case studies in Section IV demonstrate, large positions of liquid foreign currency assets can increase the resilience of dollarized banking systems both because they may be a source of emergency liquidity, and because these assets typically continue to perform in the event of a domestic shock. Since commercial banks' own foreign exchange resources are often not sufficient, central banks have in many cases acted as lender of last resort—with moral hazard implications. Figure 3.15 relates potential short-term foreign exchange claims (including deposits) to available liquidity buffers, including from the public sector's balance

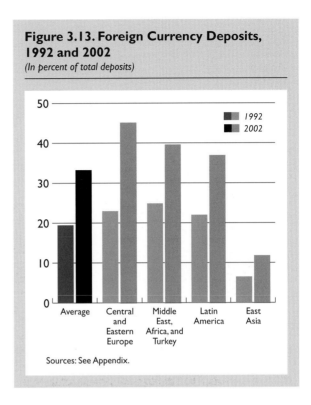

Figure 3.13. Foreign Currency Deposits, 1992 and 2002
(In percent of total deposits)

Sources: See Appendix.

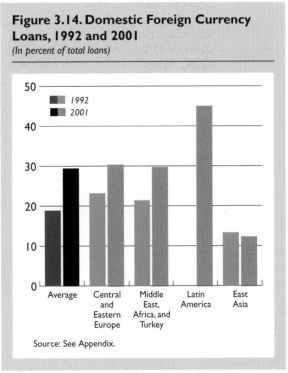

Figure 3.14. Domestic Foreign Currency Loans, 1992 and 2001
(In percent of total loans)

Source: See Appendix.

sheet. The above-mentioned buildup of official reserves has generally improved the ability to cover potential drains, especially in Asia. Latin America is again the exception.

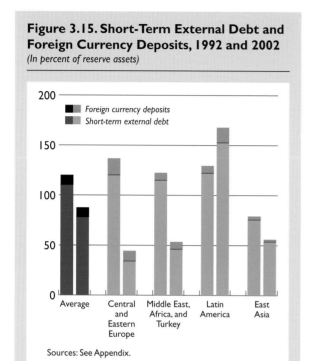

Figure 3.15. Short-Term External Debt and Foreign Currency Deposits, 1992 and 2002
(In percent of reserve assets)

Sources: See Appendix.

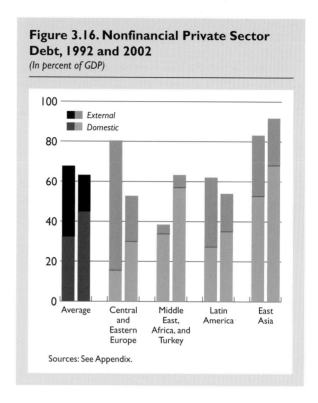

Figure 3.16. Nonfinancial Private Sector Debt, 1992 and 2002
(In percent of GDP)

Sources: See Appendix.

The Nonfinancial Private Sector's Balance Sheet

In the nonfinancial private sector, as elsewhere, domestic debt has been replacing external debt.[22] The average external debt level across regions more than halved from 40 percent to less that 20 percent of GDP, falling markedly in all regions except in the Middle East, Africa, and Turkey group (Figure 3.16). At the same time, loans from the domestic banking sector rose from 30 percent to 45 percent of GDP, leaving the average overall debt level almost unchanged.

Because a high share of domestic debt is denominated in foreign currency, the sector's exposure to various market risks remains substantial. In 2001, the average amount of foreign currency debt still amounted to over 30 percent of GDP—somewhat more than in 1994—of which only two-thirds constituted debt owed to nonresidents (Figure 3.17).[23] This foreign-currency-denominated domestic debt, which is the flip side of the rise in banks' foreign currency loans described earlier, creates a vulnerability to currency risk among indebted households and firms.

Moreover, there is evidence that it combines with rollover risk: while the overall level of the private sector's (banks and corporations) external debt on average fell by more than half, short-term external debt declined by less than one-third. This is probably the result of an increased share of external trade credit (which typically is short term), as trade flows have increased and longer-term project financing is increasingly derived from domestic sources.

External assets of the nonfinancial private sector have decreased overall. Figure 3.18 shows holdings of households and corporations in banks of BIS-reporting countries. While indicative of trends, this excludes a number of important financial centers (e.g., those offshore) and the average again conceals some regional disparities. Specifically, the fall in average assets is driven by very large decreases in two countries—Lebanon and Panama, in the former case presumably driven by repatriations in the postwar reconstruction period. Excluding these countries, external assets in both Latin America and the Middle East, and the sample as a whole, increased slightly.

As regards external flows of the nonfinancial private sector, the ratio of foreign currency debt to exports and remittances has increased slightly from 85 percent in 1994 to 90 percent in 2001 (Figure 3.19), though there are large regional discrepancies. While the ratio fell substantially in both East Asia and Cen-

---

[22]Unless otherwise noted, the nonfinancial private sector includes households and corporations.

[23]Data for a sufficiently large sample of countries were not available for 1992.

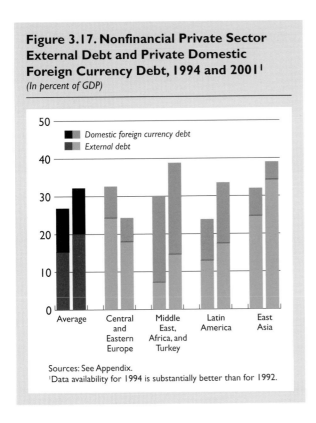

Figure 3.17. Nonfinancial Private Sector External Debt and Private Domestic Foreign Currency Debt, 1994 and 2001[1]
(In percent of GDP)

Sources: See Appendix.
[1]Data availability for 1994 is substantially better than for 1992.

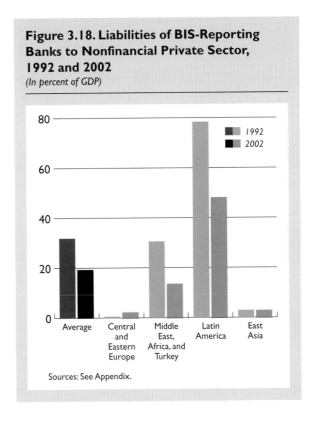

Figure 3.18. Liabilities of BIS-Reporting Banks to Nonfinancial Private Sector, 1992 and 2002
(In percent of GDP)

Sources: See Appendix.

tral and Eastern Europe, it increased in Latin America—from already very high levels—and Middle East, Africa, and Turkey, the latter largely on account of Lebanon, where foreign exchange loans increased strongly over the period. Corporations and households that have no direct foreign currency earnings are a particular source of risk to banks in the event of a depreciation of the exchange rate. This is especially true for households, which have only limited access to hedging and foreign exchange earnings (except remittances).

Currency forward markets may provide corporations the opportunity to hedge their exchange rate risk. In many of the more advanced emerging market economies, markets for currency forwards or swaps exist in which corporations without sufficient foreign currency receipts can hedge their exposure. Such off-balance-sheet transactions can help to distribute the risk to those entities that can best cope with it; for example, corporations with strong export revenues, banks with long dollar positions, or the public sector. Brazil, described in detail in the next section, provides an example of the latter. But for the economy as a whole, such operations can only be effective if they involve nonresidents as ultimate providers of short foreign exchange exposure. Otherwise, the risk is only shifted from one balance sheet to the other within the economy.

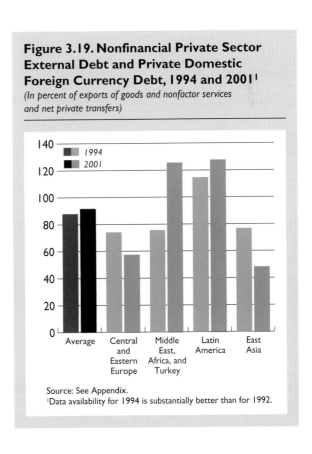

Figure 3.19. Nonfinancial Private Sector External Debt and Private Domestic Foreign Currency Debt, 1994 and 2001[1]
(In percent of exports of goods and nonfactor services and net private transfers)

Source: See Appendix.
[1]Data availability for 1994 is substantially better than for 1992.

Figure 3.20. Economy-Wide Vulnerabilities, Emerging Market Countries, 1992, 1997, and 2002

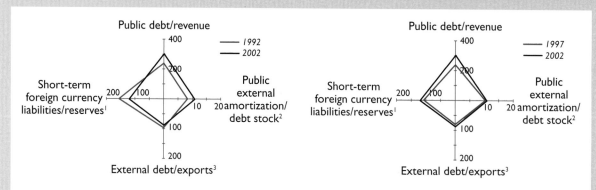

Sources: See Appendix.
[1]Reserves are the stock of gross reserves and foreign assets of the banking system. Assumes no net open currency position in the banking sector.
[2]Public and publicly guaranteed medium- and long-term external debt.
[3]The sum of exports of goods and nonfactor services and net private transfers in the given and prior year.

Figure 3.21. Economy-Wide Vulnerabilities, Regional, 1992 and 2002

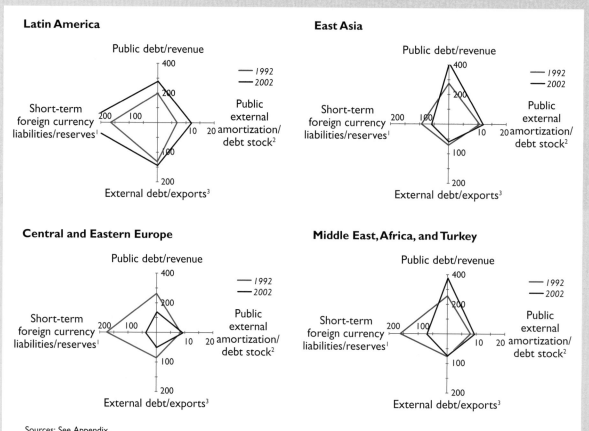

Sources: See Appendix.
[1]Reserves are the stock of gross reserves and foreign assets of the banking system. Assumes no net open currency position in the banking sector.
[2]Public and publicly guaranteed medium- and long-term external debt.
[3]The sum of exports of goods and nonfactor services and net private transfers in the given and prior year.

Presenting Economy-Wide Vulnerabilities

Some of the key indicators of sectoral vulnerabilities can be summarized in a diamond-shaped figure. In principle, any of the measures of vulnerability in the public or private sector discussed above can be used. For illustration, Figures 3.20 to 3.22 present some well-known metrics, which include the following:

- Public debt as a share of revenue, as a proxy for public debt sustainability;

- Short-term external debt (amortizations in one year) as a share of public sector debt, as a gauge of rollover risk in the public sector;

- External debt as a share of exports, as a proxy of external sustainability; and

- Short-term debt and domestic foreign currency deposits over reserves, as a more comprehensive measure of rollover risk (including that related to domestic depositors) and currency risk.[24]

For all regions taken together, some vulnerabilities have increased as others have declined over the last decade. In the past five years, however, vulnera-

bilities have unambiguously increased. In the example shown in Figure 3.20, the left panel shows the situation in 2002 compared to 1992; the right panel compares 2002 with 1997.

Between 1992 and 2002, public sector debt sustainability and rollover risks deteriorated. On the other hand, the risk of combined currency and liquidity crises has diminished, if one assumes that the public sector is prepared to use the recent surge of its official reserves to provide emergency liquidity support. The comparison between the situations in 1997 and 2002 illustrates that in conducting this kind of analysis, the choice of base year matters—worldwide vulnerabilities unambiguously increased in the later part of the 1990s, reflecting a series of financial crises that negatively affected a number of countries in the sample.

Important differences emerge across regions and between countries that experienced a crisis and those that did not. While Central and Eastern Europe has clearly become less vulnerable, Latin America appears more crisis-prone at the end of 2002, especially with regard to its public debt (see Figure 3.21). Vulnerabilities have unambiguously increased in countries that experienced a crisis during the last decade, as their public balance sheets were damaged by loss of market access, devaluation, and forced bank recapitalization (Figure 3.22). In noncrisis countries, by contrast, some vulnerabilities were reduced, in particular regarding the reserve coverage of short-term foreign currency liabilities. The case

---

[24]Since March 2003, Moody's has been using such an index in its ratings methodology.

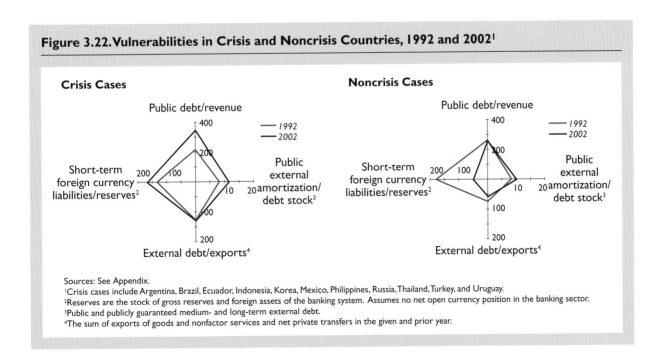

Figure 3.22. Vulnerabilities in Crisis and Noncrisis Countries, 1992 and 2002[1]

Sources: See Appendix.
[1]Crisis cases include Argentina, Brazil, Ecuador, Indonesia, Korea, Mexico, Philippines, Russia, Thailand, Turkey, and Uruguay.
[2]Reserves are the stock of gross reserves and foreign assets of the banking system. Assumes no net open currency position in the banking sector.
[3]Public and publicly guaranteed medium- and long-term external debt.
[4]The sum of exports of goods and nonfactor services and net private transfers in the given and prior year.

studies in the next section further highlight balance sheet developments in crisis and noncrisis countries.

Caution is in order when interpreting any such set of vulnerability indicators. The comparison between 1992 and 2002 may overlook recent trends, and the choice of indicators may not capture important balance sheet vulnerabilities. For example, the unequivocal improvement in Central and Eastern Europe, as measured by the metrics chosen, could well mask the risks associated with the credit booms, current account widenings, and rigid exchange rate regimes recently observed in some of these countries. The purpose of Figures 3.20–3.22 is, therefore, not to assess the present probability of crises in individual countries or regions—this is done much more accurately in the IMF's internal vulnerability exercise—but rather to propose a way of presenting balance sheet risks across time and countries.

Appendix. Regional Groupings and Data Sources and Definitions

A. Regional Groupings

Region	Countries
Central and Eastern Europe	Bulgaria Croatia Hungary Poland Russia Slovak Republic Ukraine
East Asia	Indonesia Korea Malaysia Philippines Thailand
Latin America	Argentina Brazil Colombia Ecuador Mexico Panama Uruguay República Bolivariana de Venezuela
Middle East, Africa, and Turkey	Egypt Lebanon Morocco South Africa Turkey

B. Data Sources and Definitions

Figure	Sources and Definitions	Missing Observations
Figure 3.1.	IMF, Fiscal Affairs Department, and IMF (2003c) for Slovak Republic.	For 1992: Colombia, Croatia, Egypt, Panama, Russia, Slovak Republic, Thailand, and Ukraine.
Figure 3.2.	IMF, Fiscal Affairs Department.	For 1992: Colombia, Croatia, Egypt, Hungary, Lebanon, Panama, Russia, Slovak Republic, Thailand, and Ukraine. For 2002: Slovak Republic.
Figure 3.3.	IMF staff estimates.	For 2002: Slovak Republic.
Figure 3.4.	World Bank, *Global Development Finance*. Private = [public and publicly guaranteed (PPG) medium- and long-term (MLT) external debt owed to private creditors]/(total PPG MLT external debt)*100. Public = 1 − private.	For 1992: Croatia and South Africa.
Figure 3.5.	IMF staff estimates. Maturity = (total PPG MLT external debt)/(PPG MLT external amortization for current plus prior year).	For 1991: Croatia, South Africa, and Ukraine.
Figure 3.6.	J.P. Morgan (2002).	For 2001: Argentina, Bulgaria, Colombia, Croatia, Ecuador, Egypt, Korea, Lebanon, Morocco, Panama, Russia, Ukraine, and Uruguay.
Figure 3.7.	IMF, World Economic Outlook database and as calculated in IMF debt sustainability templates.	For 1992: Argentina, Hungary, Panama, and Slovak Republic. For 2002: Argentina, Hungary, Panama, and Slovak Republic.
Figure 3.8.	IMF, World Economic Outlook database, and IMF staff estimates for Turkey, Korea, Malaysia, Philippines, and Thailand in 2002. Primary surplus = (primary balance/exchange rate)/GDP*100.	For 1992: Korea, Malaysia, Philippines, Thailand, and Ukraine.
Figure 3.9.	IMF, Fiscal Affairs Department for debt and World Economic Outlook database for other. Public external debt/exports = [(external debt in percent of GDP/100)*World Economic Outlook database GDP]/[(exports of goods and nonfactor services + net total transfers − net official transfers)/exchange rate]*100.	For 1992: Colombia, Croatia, Egypt, Hungary, Lebanon, Panama, Russia, Slovak Republic, Thailand, and Ukraine. For 2002: Slovak Republic.
Figure 3.10.	IMF, *International Financial Statistics* for use of IMF credit and World Economic Outlook database for other. Gross reserves = stock of reserves at year-end/GDP*100. Net reserves = [(stock of reserves at year-end) − (use of IMF credit)]/GDP*100.	For 1992: Slovak Republic.
Figure 3.11.	IMF, World Economic Outlook database for GDP and exchange rate and *International Financial Statistics* for other. Banking sector assets/GDP = [(Reserves + foreign assets + claims on central government + claims on state and local governments + claims on nonfinancial public enterprises + claims on private sector + claims on other banking institutions + claims on nonbank financial institutions)/exchange rate]/GDP*100.	For 1992: Argentina, Bulgaria, Croatia, Malaysia, Russia, and Slovak Republic. For 2002: Ecuador.
Figure 3.12.	IMF, World Economic Outlook database for GDP and *International Financial Statistics* for other. Public = (claims on central government + claims on state and local governments + claims on nonfinancial public enterprises)/exchange rate. Private = (claims on private sector)/exchange rate.	For 1992: Argentina, Croatia, Russia, and Slovak Republic. For 2002: Ecuador and Slovak Republic. For 1992: Croatia, Russia, and Slovak Republic. For 2002: Ecuador.

B. Data Sources and Definitions *(continued)*

Figure	Sources and Definitions	Missing Observations
Figure 3.13.	De Nicoló, Honohan, and Ize (2003), and IMF staff estimates for Brazil.	For 1992: Colombia, Croatia, Hungary, Lebanon, Malaysia, Mexico, Morocco, Panama, Philippines, Poland, Russia, Slovak Republic, Uruguay, and Venezuela
		For 2002: Colombia, Hungary, Morocco, Panama, and Slovak Republic.
Figure 3.14.	De Nicoló, Honohan, and Ize (2003).	For 2002: All Latin American countries, Croatia, Egypt Lebanon, Malaysia, Morocco, Philippines, Poland, Russia, Slovak Republic, South Africa, Thailand, and Ukraine.
Figure 3.15.	IMF, *International Financial Statistics* for foreign assets and World Economic Outlook database for other. Short-term foreign currency debt = (total short-term debt of the economy outstanding, remaining maturity)/[(stock of reserves at year-end) + (foreign assets/exchange rate)]*100.	For 1992: Colombia, Hungary, Korea, Morocco, Panama, and Slovak Republic. For 2002: Brazil, Colombia, Croatia, Ecuador, Morocco, Panama, and Philippines.
	Foreign currency deposits = (demand deposits/exchange rate)*(share of foreign currency deposits in total)/[(stock of reserves at year-end) + (foreign assets/exchange rate)]*100.	For 1992: Colombia, Croatia, Hungary, Korea, Lebanon, Malaysia, Mexico, Morocco, Panama, Philippines, Poland, Russia, Slovak Republic, Uruguay, and Venezuela. For 2002: Colombia, Hungary, Korea, Morocco, Panama, and Slovak Republic.
Figure 3.16.	IMF, *International Financial Statistics* for claims on private sector and World Economic Outlook database for other. Domestic = (claims on the private sector/exchange rate)/GDP*100.	For 1992: Croatia, Russia, and Slovak Republic.
	External = external debt outstanding by private debtors at year-end/GDP*100.	For 1992: Korea and Poland. For 2002: Korea.
Figure 3.17.	IMF, World Economic Outlook database for debt and Fiscal Affairs Department for 1992 debt for Argentina, Brazil, Ecuador, Indonesia, Mexico, Uruguay, and Venezuela; IMF, *International Financial Statistics* for claims on the private sector. De Nicoló, Honohan, and Ize (2003) for foreign currency loans in percent of total loans.	
	External = [(total external debt outstanding at year-end) − (debt outstanding to official debtors)]/GDP*100.	For 1994: Brazil, Bulgaria, Croatia, Indonesia, Korea, Panama, Poland, and Ukraine. For 2001: Brazil, Hungary, Korea, and Poland.
	Domestic foreign currency debt = [(claims on the private sector)/exchange rate*(foreign currency loans in percent of total loans)]/GDP*100.	For 1994: Brazil, Colombia, Ecuador, Egypt, Malaysia, Morocco, Panama, Philippines, Poland, Russia, South Africa, Thailand, Ukraine, Uruguay, and Venezuela. For 2001: Brazil, Colombia, Croatia, Ecuador, Morocco, Panama, and Philippines.
Figure 3.18.	Bank for International Settlements (BIS) for liabilities; and IMF, World Economic Outlook database for GDP. Total external liabilities of BIS-reporting banks/GDP*100.	
Figure 3.19.	IMF, World Economic Outlook database. As in Figure 3.17, but denominated by: [(exports of goods and nonfactor services + net total transfers − net official transfers)/ (exchange rate)]*100.	For 1994 and 2001: As in Figure 3.17.

B. Data Sources and Definitions (concluded)

Figure	Sources and Definitions	Missing Observations
Figure 3.20, Figure 3.21, and Figure 3.22	IMF, Fiscal Affairs Department and World Economic Outlook database; and World Bank, *Global Development Finance*.	
	Public debt/revenue = (public debt in percent of GDP)/{[(revenue/exchange rate)/GDP]*100}*100.	For 1992: Colombia, Croatia, Egypt, Korea, Panama, Russia, Slovak Republic, Thailand, and Ukraine.
		For 2002: Colombia, Croatia, Egypt, Korea, Panama, Russia, Slovak Republic, Thailand, and Ukraine.
	Short-term foreign currency liabilities/reserves = (short-term external debt + foreign currency deposits)/ reserve assets*100.	For 1992: Colombia, Croatia, Egypt, Korea, Panama, Russia, Slovak Republic, Thailand, and Ukraine.
		For 2002: Colombia, Croatia, Egypt, Korea, Panama, Russia, Slovak Republic, Thailand, and Ukraine.
	External debt/exports = (total external debt outstanding at year-end)/[(exports of goods and nonfactor services + net total transfers – net official transfers)/(exchange rate)]*100.	For 1992: Korea.
		For 2002: Korea.
	Amortization/debt stock = (average of amortization of PPG MLT external debt for current and prior year)/ (stock of PPG MLT external debt)*100.	For 1992: Croatia, Slovak Republic, and South Africa.
		For 2002: Croatia, Slovak Republic, and South Africa.

IV   Balance Sheet Developments in Recent Financial Crises: Some Case Studies

This section takes a closer look at some recent crisis and near-crisis episodes in emerging market countries. The purpose is to show how an analysis of sectoral balance sheet relationships can help explain why some countries have experienced financial crises, while others have not. None of the country experiences detailed below is intended to represent an exhaustive account of that particular crisis, especially macroeconomic developments and the authorities' fiscal and monetary policies, which are well documented elsewhere. Rather, each example focuses on one salient feature of a country's experience that can be best understood by looking at it through the prism of the BSA.

Argentina: How Weaknesses in Private Sector Balance Sheets Contributed to the Crisis of 2001–02

The causes of Argentina's crisis extended to weaknesses in the private sector's balance sheets. Most attention has rightly focused on inconsistencies between Argentina's fiscal and exchange rate policies, its difficulties carrying out sufficient fiscal adjustment during a prolonged recession, and weaknesses in the public sector balance sheet, especially the government's large stock of foreign currency debt. However, these problems, which have been discussed in past IMF staff papers, were compounded by the poor management of bank and corporate balance sheets in the context of the pegged exchange rate. The BSA can help to explain how vulnerabilities in the private sector augmented the underlying weaknesses in Argentina's public sector and contributed to the depth of its crisis in 2001–02.

Currency mismatches in the private sector were severe. The private sector's foreign-currency-denominated debt was larger, in relation to exports, than in the late-1990s Asian crisis cases, crises that famously originated outside the government. This is partly due to Argentina's lower export-to-GDP ratio, but also because its banks needed to lend in foreign currency to match their domestic foreign currency deposits, adding to the mismatch created by external borrowing

(Table 4.1).[25] At the end of 2000, Argentine firms had borrowed US$37 billion externally and are estimated to have borrowed an additional US$30 billion in foreign currency from the domestic banking system—a large exposure in relation to Argentina's US$31 billion in annual exports of goods and services.[26]

Resident banks' foreign-currency-denominated lending left them exposed to a devaluation even if the government could have avoided outright default. The real burden of the dollar-denominated debts of private firms was sure to increase if either the currency board could not be sustained or a period of prolonged deflation was needed to bring about the necessary real exchange rate adjustment.[27] As in Asia, the financial difficulties of private firms in turn would weaken the banking system. Moreover, the small size of Argentina's export sector meant that there were few sellers of protection against exchange rate shocks, making it difficult for the private sector to hedge.[28]

Argentina lost more reserves in 2001 as a result of a bank run than as a result of the government's inability to access external markets to meet its financing needs. This was due to the fact that the foreign currency maturity mismatch in the banking sector was larger than in the public sector. Convertibility allowed depositors to exit at par by withdrawing pesos from the banking system, converting these pesos to dollars, and moving their funds offshore. In contrast, the relatively long

---

[25]Given the relatively small size of the tradables sector and the high degree of dollarization, the convertibility regime left banks with few other options. Nevertheless, this mismatch might have been reduced, but not eliminated, if banks had instead invested foreign currency deposits in low-risk externally issued securities.

[26]Although Argentina's supervisory and regulatory frameworks were viewed as some of the strongest in the region prior to the crisis, prudential indicators failed to take account of the banking sector's increasing exposure to the nontradables sector.

[27]Roubini (2001).

[28]Some privatized utilities had the ability to index their local prices to the dollar and to raise prices in line with U.S. inflation. This protected against both real depreciation through falling domestic prices and a nominal depreciation—but the viability of such a hedge hinged on the political will to pass the currency mismatch on to the utilities' consumers. In 2002, after the devaluation, the government decided to freeze utility prices, which broke this regulatory hedge.

Table 4.1. Argentina: Foreign-Currency-Denominated Debt of the Corporate Sector
(In billions of U.S. dollars, unless otherwise indicated)

Corporate Foreign Currency Debt	Argentina 2000	Thailand 1996	Korea 1996	Brazil 2001	Uruguay 2001
Foreign currency debt to domestic banks[1]	30.1	32.1	32.0	21.4	5.3
Foreign currency debt to external creditors	36.9	61.8	28.3	69.8	1.2
Total foreign currency debt	67.0	93.9	60.3	91.2	6.5
Exports (goods and services)	31.4	71.4	153.4	67.6	3.3
GDP	284.2	180.1	495.7	517.3	18.6
Foreign currency debt to exports (in percent)	213	132	39	135	199
Foreign currency debt to GDP (in percent)	24	52	12	18	35
External foreign currency debt to exports (in percent)	118	87	18	103	37
External foreign currency debt to GDP (in percent)	13	34	6	13	6
External debt of banking system and firms	61	114	94	108	...
In percent of GDP	21	63	19	21	...
In percent of exports	194	160	61	159	...
Memorandum items					
Domestic foreign currency deposits	48.5	...	...	...	5.2
External debt of the banking system[2]	24.1	52.1	65.9	37.9	...
External assets of the banking system	...	...	33.9	16.5	...
Stock of government foreign currency debt sold as hedge	...	...	...	73.6	...

Sources: Argentina: country authorities; Thailand: Allen and others (2002); Korea: Bank for International Settlements and IMF staff estimates; Brazil: country authorities for external debt data and IMF staff estimates; and Uruguay: Central Bank of Uruguay for domestic data and IMF, *World Economic Outlook*, for external debt data.

[1]For Brazil and Korea, upper-bound estimates (external debt of banking system – external assets).

[2]For Thailand, includes debt of finance companies.

average maturity of the government's own debt limited the pace at which international investors could reduce their exposure to the government. Of course, the bank run was not independent of the government's own financial difficulties. The government's inability to access external markets and other signs of the public sector's financial distress clearly helped to trigger a series of domestic bank runs during the course of 2001, in part because depositors remembered how previous financial crises had led to deposit freezes. The use of short-term deposits to fund long-term lending to the public sector resulted in a maturity mismatch that created a substantial vulnerability for the Argentine economy.

A simplified balance sheet that focuses on the Argentine banking system's principal assets and liabilities illustrates the impact of the bank run (Table 4.2). Domestic deposits and external liabilities fell by some US$24 billion (9 percent of GDP) during 2001. The need to finance this run forced the banking system to reduce its lending to private firms (US$12 billion), to run down its stock of liquid assets (US$5 billion) and, in the end, borrow from the central bank (US$9 billion). Deposits denominated in domestic currency fell more rapidly than those denominated in foreign currency, forcing the banking system to run down domestic-currency-denominated lending faster than its foreign-currency-denominated lending to remain matched.

This balance sheet also illustrates how the financial health of the banking system depended on the government. Claims on the public sector accounted for a significant share of the banking system's assets, linking the banks' soundness to that of the government. At the end of 2000, credit to the public sector constituted 28 percent of the principal assets of the banking system, and 35 percent of its foreign-currency-denominated assets.[29]

---

[29]The banking system's claims on the public sector at the end of 2000 reflected sharp increases in this exposure during 1999. Argentina fell into recession after a series of external shocks (the crisis in Russia and Brazil) in late 1998 and early 1999. The year 1999 also was an election year. Both the central and the provincial governments turned to the banks to fund countercyclical fiscal policy that they had difficulty financing externally. As a result, banks' net exposure to the public sector increased by US$4.7 billion in 1999 even as net external bond financing fell by US$4.5 billion. This increase in exposure initially reflected a considered balancing by banks of perceived risks against the attractive returns available on government paper. The government later exercised moral suasion on the banks to further increase their exposure as the crisis progressed.

Table 4.2. Argentina: Principal Assets and Liabilities of the Banking System
(In billions of U.S. dollars)

	End-1998	End-1999	End-2000	End-2001
Principal assets				
Cash and liquid assets	8.4	8.4	8.3	3.4
Domestic currency	2.9	2.8	2.5	1.9
Foreign currency and liquid assets	5.5	5.6	5.9	1.5
Loans to and securities issued by the public sector	23.5	28.2	28.7	30.1
Domestic currency	4.8	5.5	3.7	3.4
Foreign currency	18.7	22.7	25.0	26.7
Loans to and securities issued by the private sector	70.5	68.4	65.8	54.2
Domestic currency	26.9	25.9	25.0	15.0
Foreign currency	43.7	42.5	40.9	39.1
Subtotals				
Domestic currency assets	34.5	34.2	31.2	20.3
Foreign currency assets	68.0	70.8	71.7	67.3
Total assets	102.5	105.0	102.9	87.6
Principal liabilities				
Deposits	77.3	79.9	83.2	67.3
Domestic currency	37.3	35.8	34.7	21.7
Foreign currency	40.0	44.2	48.5	45.6
External obligations	21.4	22.8	24.1	16.3
Domestic currency	0.5	0.5	0.4	0.1
Foreign currency	20.9	22.2	23.7	16.2
Subtotals				
Domestic currency liabilities	37.8	36.3	35.1	21.7
Foreign currency liabilities	60.9	66.4	72.2	61.8
Total liabilities	98.7	102.7	107.3	83.5
Central bank support	0.3	0.2	0.1	9.2
Domestic currency	0.3	0.2	0.0	4.1
Foreign currency[1]	...	...	0.1	5.1
Liabilities, including liabilities to central bank	99.0	103.0	107.5	92.7

Source: Central Bank of Argentina presentation based on Lagos (2002).

[1]Data from Lagos (2002). Central Bank of Argentina (BCRA) swap obligations disaggregated from other obligations due to financial intermediation in BCRA data.

The government was in no position in 2001 to help the banks manage a run—to the contrary, it was looking to the banking system for help to manage its own liquidity shortage. The government needed to refinance US$19.3 billion in maturing debt, including US$5.8 billion in payments to external bondholders, as well as to finance its ongoing deficit. The government could not draw on the central bank's reserves to help meet its own liquidity needs, owing to the currency board, and it lacked its own stock of reserve assets; it therefore needed the domestic banking system both to roll over its maturing claims on the government and to supply the government with additional financing.[30]

However, the ongoing flight of bank deposits constrained the banking system's ability to help finance the government, particularly after the first quarter of 2001.

The ability of the banking system to withstand a twin shock of default and devaluation was substantially reduced by the need to finance deposit outflows during 2001. The banks could not reduce their exposure to the government to help finance the deposit outflow without triggering a crisis. Consequently, they had to draw down their own external assets to finance both the deposit outflow and the fall in external credit lines (and, to a lesser ex-

---

[30]The government also looked to domestic pension funds for financial assistance. These funds were investing a large fraction of

new inflows in new government debt issues and, in the context of a large-scale swap operation in June 2001, agreed to capitalize all interest payments on their existing holdings of long-term bonds.

Figure 4.1. Argentina: Maturity Mismatches: With and Without Foreign Currency Deposits, 2001
(In billions of U.S. dollars)

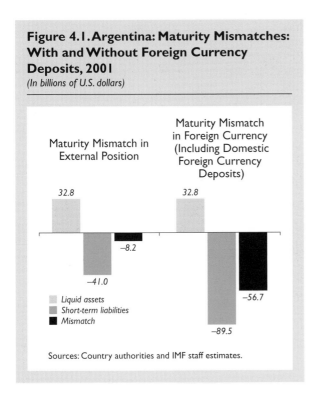

Maturity Mismatch in External Position

Maturity Mismatch in Foreign Currency (Including Domestic Foreign Currency Deposits)

32.8

32.8

−8.2

−41.0

−56.7

−89.5

Liquid assets
Short-term liabilities
Mismatch

Sources: Country authorities and IMF staff estimates.

tent, to finance a small increase in banks' aggregate exposure to the government). This eliminated an asset that would have continued to perform in the event of default and devaluation. The banks also had to cut their loans denominated in domestic currency to remain matched, even though such loans were more likely to continue to perform in the event of a devaluation than foreign currency loans. As the banking system shrank in the face of the run, an increasing share of banks' remaining assets became illiquid foreign-currency-denominated claims on the government (US$26.7 billion at the end of 2001) and on firms that lacked sufficient export revenue to finance these claims (US$39.1 billion at the end of 2001). Overall, the currency maturity mismatch was substantial (Figure 4.1).

The changes in the balance sheet of the banking system during the course of 2001 illustrate the costs of delaying a debt restructuring. It is unclear if banks could have withstood the shock of a restructuring and devaluation at the end of 2000, but the chances of avoiding a generalized banking crisis declined substantially during the course of 2001. This is not to say that government recourse to banks was necessarily wrong ex ante. The dangers of weakening the banks' balance sheets to help tide a cash-strapped government through a crisis had to be traded off against the need to tap all available sources of financing to prevent a deepening of the crisis.

The authorities ended up addressing Argentina's internal balance sheet mismatch through pesification:[31] in 2003, both the banks' liabilities and their assets were converted into local currency, though at different rates. While the banking system's assets were converted at parity, liabilities were exchanged at 1.4 pesos for each U.S. dollar. This allowed nonperforming dollar assets to be quickly replaced with performing peso assets. Although nonperforming assets did reemerge, pesification likely dampened the debt-servicing difficulties that would have resulted if these private sector debts to the banks had remained denominated in U.S. dollars. Pesification also allowed the central bank to supply large amounts of liquidity support to the banking system. But like all across-the-board solutions, pesification traded equity for efficiency—and prior to the issuance of compensation bonds to close most of the financial losses created by pesification, the asymmetric rates at which the banking system's assets and liabilities were pesified also imposed large losses on banks' shareholders. The issuance of compensation bonds, though, added to the government's domestic debt burden and further weakened its own balance sheet.

Argentina demonstrates how close examination of domestic balance sheets can highlight key vulnerabilities, particularly when combined with readily available external debt data. Two insights stand out. First, the banking system's foreign currency exposure to the private sector substantially exceeded its exposure to the government. Rather than being a source of strength, this was a potential weakness, given the small size of the export sector and extensive lending to firms in the nontradables sector. Any government debt crisis that resulted in a devaluation was therefore likely to be combined with an Asian-style bank-corporate crisis. Second, drawing on the banking system to help tide the government through a liquidity crisis can increase the risk of a deposit run, and particularly in the context of a fixed exchange rate, may lead to very large reserve losses. In highlighting these additional facets of the crisis in Argentina, the balance sheet approach underscores the role played by domestic private sector balance sheet mismatches in augmenting Argentina's vulnerabilities.

---

[31]External debts could not be pesified. Both the government of Argentina and many Argentine firms are in the process of renegotiating their external debt. The government is servicing its domestic peso debts even though it remains in default on a portion of its external debt. A debt exchange completed in June 2005 regularized relations with about 76 percent of Argentina's external bondholders. Firms, however, cannot pay their domestic creditors while they are in default on their external debt. Many firms consequently have been putting funds into domestic escrow accounts.

Uruguay: How a Run on Banks Led to the Sovereign Debt Crisis of 2002

Uruguay's 2002 financial crisis began with a run by liquidity-constrained Argentine nationals on nonresident foreign currency deposits. While the crisis is sometimes, therefore, seen as a pure product of contagion that gained momentum when the Uruguayan exchange rate regime was loosened in June 2002, a simplified balance sheet analysis highlights the crucial role that asymmetries in the Uruguayan banking sector played in raising doubts about the government's capacity both to service its debt and to support the banking system. Such doubts led to the loss of Uruguay's investment-grade status and eventually forced the liquidity-constrained government to undertake a preemptive debt restructuring. This section traces how Uruguay's crisis cascaded from the financial sector to the public sector's balance sheet.

Uruguay's relatively strong economic performance throughout the 1990s masked an accumulation of balance sheet weaknesses in the banking sector. With total bank deposits at about 90 percent of GDP, Uruguay's banking system was large for an emerging economy of its size. At the end of 2001 the sector was marked by the following characteristics:

- *A high degree of dollarization.* At the end of 2001, about 80 percent of deposits and over 70 percent of loans were denominated in U.S. dollars (Figure 4.2).

- *Substantial nonresident deposits.* Nonresident deposits, mainly from Argentina, accounted for nearly half of total liabilities (Table 4.3). Most of these deposits were denominated in U.S. dollars.

- *Relatively balanced system-wide external foreign currency assets and liabilities.* Total nonresident borrowing amounted to US$6.6 billion, which, combined with US$1.4 billion in foreign reserves deposited at the central bank, broadly matched the US$7.9 billion in nonresident foreign currency deposits (Figure 4.3). Nevertheless, the quality of these assets was not uniform and, in practice, the match of external foreign currency assets and liabilities may not have been as clear as this accounting exercise implies.

- *A substantial system-wide foreign currency liquidity mismatch.* Liquid foreign currency assets mostly covered nonresident foreign currency deposits, but were not enough to cover also concurrent withdrawals of foreign currency by resident depositors (Figure 4.4).

- *A relatively large liquidity mismatch in the onshore banking system.*[32] Compared with the offshore banking sector, where foreign currency liquidity was relatively well matched (Figure 4.5), there was a substantial imbalance in the onshore banking system. Within the onshore banking system, mismatches in the foreign-owned banks were, relative to the size of their respective deposit bases, broadly similar to those of Uruguayan-controlled institutions (Figure 4.6), but the latter were prone to extending medium- and long-term loans to domestic entities that often lacked foreign currency revenue streams.[33]

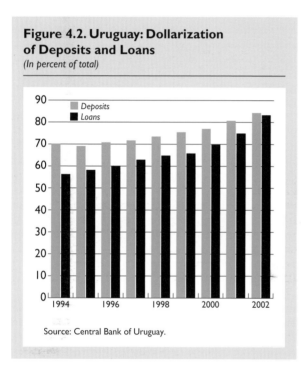

Figure 4.2. Uruguay: Dollarization of Deposits and Loans
(In percent of total)

Source: Central Bank of Uruguay.

Table 4.3. Uruguay: Deposit Structure, by Residency
(In percent of total)

	End-2000	End-2001	End-2002
Residents	56	54	63
Nonresidents	44	46	37

Source: Central Bank of Uruguay.

---

[32]No restrictions on ownership and client base exist for the onshore banking system, but the offshore banking system is licensed to operate only with nonresidents.

[33]Foreign banks may have also sought to avoid Argentina's reserve requirements by lending foreign currency back into Argentina at favorable rates. As the crisis in Argentina deepened, such assets became increasingly illiquid and/or nonperforming.

Figure 4.3. Uruguay: System-Wide Foreign Currency Balance Sheet, 2001
(In billions of U.S. dollars)

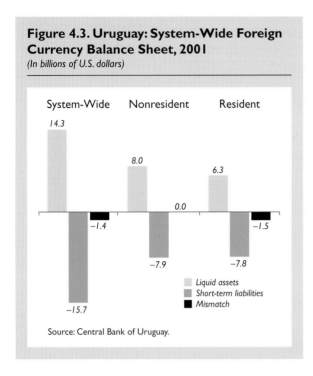

Source: Central Bank of Uruguay.

Figure 4.4. Uruguay: Maturity Mismatch and Domestic Foreign Currency Deposits, 2001
(In billions of U.S. dollars)

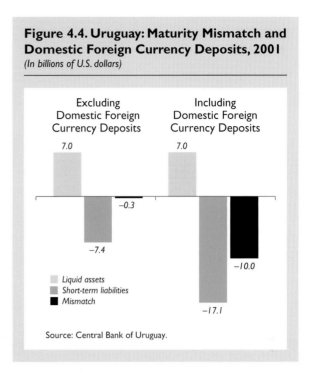

Source: Central Bank of Uruguay.

Figure 4.5. Uruguay: Foreign Currency Balance Sheets, 2001
(In billions of U.S. dollars)

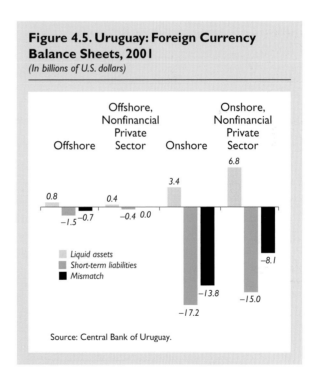

Source: Central Bank of Uruguay.

• *Weak public banks with large liquidity and currency mismatches.* About one quarter of the liquidity and currency mismatches in the onshore banking sector were related to two public banks. The public banks' implicit government guarantee provided them with little incentive to address these mismatches.

• *Limited freely available international reserves.* Although gross reserves had risen to US$3.1 billion (or 200 percent of base money and eight months of imports) by the end of 2001, freely available reserves (less deposits by banks and financial institutions at the central bank) were only US$1.4 billion (Figure 4.7), or less than 10 percent of total dollar deposits.[34] The central bank was therefore not well placed to help the banking system respond to a major shock to its liquidity.

• *Weak regulation and supervision.* There were no special liquidity requirements on either resident or nonresident deposits, no direct limits on exposure to currency risk, no quantitative limits on foreign currency lending, and no limits on maturity mismatches.

In sum, Uruguay's banking system balance sheet at the end of 2001 was highly vulnerable to the run on offshore foreign currency deposits that developed during 2002.

---

[34]If one includes banks' foreign currency deposits at the central bank, coverage of dollar deposits rises to 22 percent.

The crisis on the liability side of the banks' balance sheets escalated when residents began rapidly withdrawing their foreign currency deposits in early 2002. These outflows and the related liquidity support to banks made the Uruguayan peso's crawling band

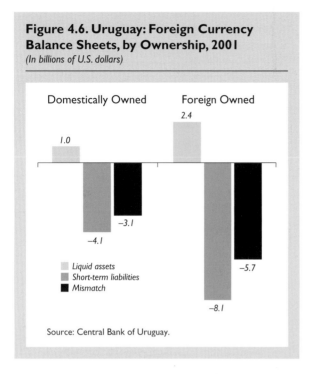

Figure 4.6. Uruguay: Foreign Currency Balance Sheets, by Ownership, 2001
(In billions of U.S. dollars)

Source: Central Bank of Uruguay.

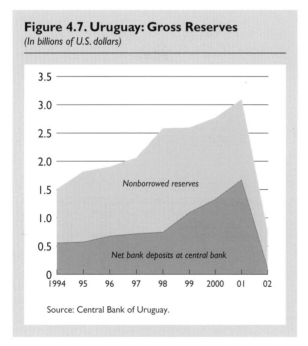

Figure 4.7. Uruguay: Gross Reserves
(In billions of U.S. dollars)

Source: Central Bank of Uruguay.

and the announcement that funds from an augmented IMF Stand-By Arrangement would provision liquidity support to a core group of domestically owned banks.

This enormous loss of deposits drained Uruguay's liquid foreign assets. Altogether, about 45 percent of the banking system's total foreign currency deposits were withdrawn from the system in 2002. About half of the run was financed by a US$2.8 billion reduction in the banking system's foreign assets and a US$0.9 billion reduction in bank reserve deposits at the central bank. Additional financing came from both the IMF's Stand-By Arrangement and the government's reserves. At the same time, nonperforming loans increased from 17 percent of total loans in 2001 to 36 percent in 2002 as the peso depreciation made it difficult for borrowers to service their U.S.-dollar-denominated debt.

Lacking the foreign currency resources to generate a smooth rollover of its debt and having lost investment-grade status in early 2002, the government was forced to undertake a preemptive debt restructuring in 2003. The cost of servicing public debt, almost all of which was denominated in U.S. dollars, increased substantially with the peso's real depreciation and, owing to both the depreciation and liquidity support to the banking system, public debt ballooned from about 54 percent of GDP at the end of 2001 to nearly 100 percent by the end of 2002 (Figure 4.8). The central bank's reserves, including purchases from the IMF, were committed to backing the banking system through, inter alia, the creation of the Fund for Stabilizing the Banking System, and could not be used to finance the government's debt or offset the risk that the government's own creditors may not refinance this debt. Consequently, Uruguay was forced to undertake a preemptive debt restructuring that provided debt-service relief, rather than debt reduction, by reprogramming obligations further into the future.[35]

Interestingly, the sovereign debt crisis did not touch off a second round of banking sector problems. There are several possible reasons: at the onset of the crisis, Uruguayan banks had little exposure to public debt (about 5 percent of assets at the end of 2001) and this was unchanged at the end of 2002. Additionally, by the time the banking system began stabilizing in August 2002, deposits had been substantially pruned, leaving few left to run in response to the sovereign restructuring. Finally, the decision to ring-fence a core set of banks and highlight the

unsustainable and it was abandoned in June 2002; the ensuing 50 percent depreciation raised concerns about the solvency of the banking system and served to accelerate the flight of foreign currency deposits from onshore banks. A bank holiday was imposed at the end of July 2002 and subsequently lifted in conjunction with a reprogramming of domestic time deposits

---

[35]The exchange did not entail a haircut, but by rolling over and lengthening the maturities of outstanding bonds at their original coupons, the exchange did provide a reduction in the net present value of the debt.

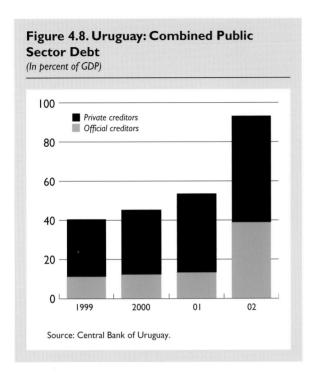

Figure 4.8. Uruguay: Combined Public Sector Debt
(In percent of GDP)

Source: Central Bank of Uruguay.

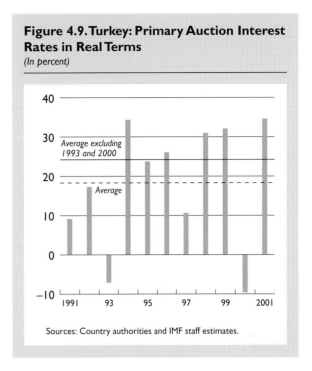

Figure 4.9. Turkey: Primary Auction Interest Rates in Real Terms
(In percent)

Sources: Country authorities and IMF staff estimates.

strength of foreign-owned institutions helped maintain confidence in these remaining banks and thus reduced the chances of further runs. The ongoing restructuring of the public banks has created significant contingent liabilities for the nonfinancial public sector, which could add to the public debt should these contingencies materialize. But the sequencing of Uruguay's financial crisis implies that, under certain circumstances, the links between an economy's sectoral balance sheets can be unidirectional.

Turkey: How Banks' Balance Sheet Positions Contributed to the Crisis of 2000–01

Exposures in the public and financial sector, and tight financial links between them, contributed to, and amplified, Turkey's twin banking and currency crisis of 2000–01. When Turkey experienced capital account pressures in November 2000, it was about ten months into an exchange-rate-based disinflation program that had shown some initial success. The reasons for these pressures—which eventually led to the floating of the currency in February 2001 and a severe output contraction—are manifold and extensively discussed elsewhere. An analysis of the public sector's financing needs in combination with the banking sector's asset-liability position in the run-up to the crisis offers valuable insights into the underlying causes of the crisis.

Throughout the 1990s, the public sector's debt structure became increasingly vulnerable. The public sector borrowing requirement rose from 10 percent of GNP to more than 20 percent in 1999, doubling the public sector debt ratio to 60 percent of GNP. Inflation averaged close to 80 percent in the 1990s[36] and high real interest rates were offered in order to place the government's lira paper (Figure 4.9). A significant share of public debt was denominated in foreign currency, and, in the wake of the Russian and Brazilian crises, the maturity of this debt progressively shortened.

The banking sector balance sheet clearly reflected this worsening economic environment. First, high inflation eroded the public's confidence in the local currency and led agents to adopt a short-term perspective. Both were evident on the liability side of banks' balance sheets: the average maturity of local currency deposits was extremely short, and over half of the deposits were held in foreign currency. Second, on the asset side, the public sector's large borrowing needs caused the crowding out of private sector credit in favor of treasury paper (Figure 4.10).

Importantly, the operations of state banks created massive distortions in the financial market. Being forced to extend preferential loans to political con-

---

[36]High and varying inflation rates pose additional problems for balance sheet analysis. The data presented in this section, especially those for the 1990s, therefore need to be interpreted with care.

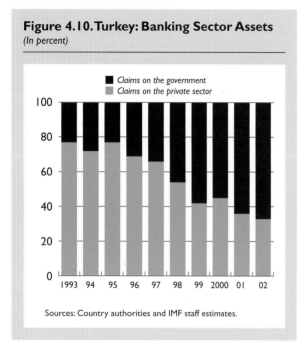

Figure 4.10. Turkey: Banking Sector Assets
(In percent)

Legend:
■ *Claims on the government*
■ *Claims on the private sector*

Sources: Country authorities and IMF staff estimates.

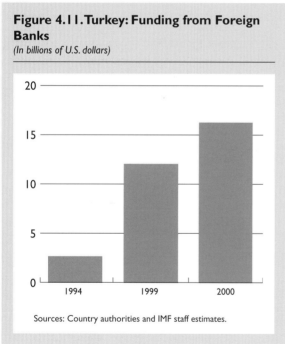

Figure 4.11. Turkey: Funding from Foreign Banks
(In billions of U.S. dollars)

Sources: Country authorities and IMF staff estimates.

stituencies and to accumulate receivables from the government (so-called duty losses), state banks' balance sheets deteriorated significantly.[37] To meet their escalating liquidity needs in the run-up to the

crisis, these banks borrowed heavily, initially from households and later in 2000 on the overnight market. This drove up interest rates, further exacerbating banks' vulnerability to liquidity and interest rate shocks.

At the same time, private banks ran large currency mismatches as they exploited the arbitrage opportunity of borrowing at low cost abroad and investing in high-yield local-currency sovereign debt. The high real interest rates on lira paper offered a lucrative carry trade, given banks' expectation that under the existing managed float the exchange rate would depreciate more or less at the rate of inflation, while the central bank would provide banks with sufficient liquidity through open market operations to ensure the rollover of government debt. This moral hazard resulted in a substantial currency mismatch on banks' balance sheets (Figure 4.11).[38]

Perversely, the initial success of the exchange-rate-based disinflation program that started in December 1999 added to the incentive to maintain large currency mismatches. The program, anchored on a predetermined exchange rate path, contributed to a sharp drop in nominal and real interest rates in the first months of 2000. In response, banks not only reduced their deposit rates, but—in expectation of a further decline—increased their holdings of longer-term fixed-rate government debt. They also sought to boost their local currency lending to the private sector, as the fiscal tightening under the program meant that they would have to diversify away from public sector assets. At the same time, the preannounced exchange rate path and the real appreciation of the Turkish lira made foreign currency funding appear even cheaper. Banks responded by borrowing more in foreign currency, thus running an even larger negative net open foreign currency position (Figure 4.12). Excluding holdings of foreign-currency-indexed assets and forwards (which to a large extent consisted of contracts with connected parties with little or no foreign exchange earnings), this open position reached more than 300 percent of bank capital on the eve of the November 2000 crisis.

This change in the composition of bank balance sheets significantly raised their liquidity, interest rate, and currency risks. First, banks were borrowing short term in foreign currency, while lending to the government in local currency, increasingly at (relatively) longer maturities. In addition to this com-

---

[37]Indeed, the two largest state banks eventually became insolvent, and a fundamental restructuring of state banks became necessary.

[38]As enforcement of regulatory limits was tightened in 2000 under the IMF-supported program, banks extended foreign-currency-indexed loans and bought forwards, which under prudential rules they were permitted to net out from their on-balance-sheet foreign currency position. While the quality of these hedges has been subject to debate, weak banking supervision, poor corporate governance, and the abuse of banks by their owners all contributed to the weakness of the banking sector.

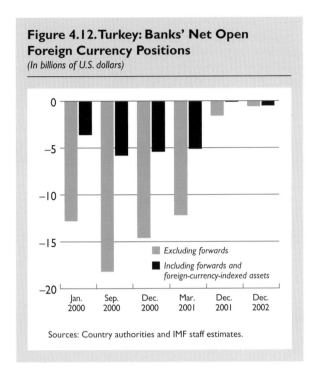

Figure 4.12. Turkey: Banks' Net Open Foreign Currency Positions
(In billions of U.S. dollars)

Sources: Country authorities and IMF staff estimates.

Under these circumstances, an interest rate defense of the exchange rate peg could not be sustained and sharp fiscal adjustment became the only available option to stem the crisis. The initial surge in interest rates in November 2000 caused a drop in the value of banks' holdings of fixed-rate government securities and simultaneously increased their short-term funding costs. The subsequent exchange rate depreciation in February 2001 fully exposed banks' negative net open foreign currency positions. In light of the banking sector's financial distress, foreign investors' confidence dwindled, adding to capital flight and associated pressures on the exchange and interest rates. Given the choice of exchange rate regime, only a sharp fiscal adjustment could alleviate these pressures.

While the public sector's fragility had contributed to the banking crisis, its own balance sheet now deteriorated sharply. The depreciation that followed the floating of the lira caused the public debt ratio to jump by about 30 percentage points of GDP (Figure 4.13). Notably, the share of domestic debt at floating rates rose significantly (Figure 4.14) because investors would only accept local currency instruments if their real value would be protected, and also because domestic banks needed assets that would reduce their interest rate exposure (which they had increased earlier in expectation of falling interest rates). Furthermore, in mid-2001, the government exchanged the equivalent of US$5 billion in lira debt for dollar-indexed

bined liquidity-currency risk, banks' interest rate risk from domestic funding also rose, because the longer-term local currency lending to the government was mostly at fixed rates, while the rates on lira demand deposits were adjusted promptly. Of course, the degree of these mismatches varied between individual banks, but when some particularly weak banks eventually failed, the fragility of the entire banking sector was revealed.

The combined public and banking sector mismatches constrained the available policy options to deal with the crisis. The government could have reduced banks' currency mismatches and eased its rollover problems by issuing foreign currency debt (as it in fact did later, as described below), but this would have increased its own currency mismatch and sharply reduced banks' profitability. On the other hand, banks could not simply be forced to reduce rapidly their currency mismatch by building up foreign currency assets, as this would have undermined the smooth rollover of government debt and put pressure on interest rates. Higher interest rates, in turn, would not only have raised doubts about the sustainability of the public debt burden, but also created further losses for the banks that had large maturity mismatches. Furthermore, a rapid elimination of banks' open positions would have created the exchange rate pressures that the IMF-supported program was precisely trying to avert. The program's crawling peg also precluded large liquidity injections by the central bank.

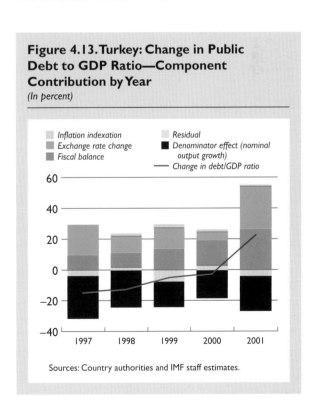

Figure 4.13. Turkey: Change in Public Debt to GDP Ratio—Component Contribution by Year
(In percent)

Sources: Country authorities and IMF staff estimates.

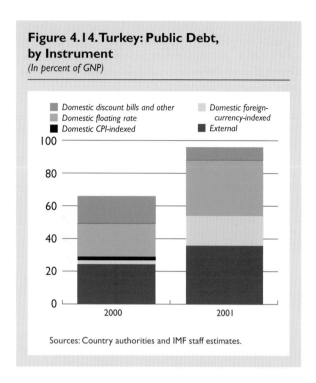

Figure 4.14. Turkey: Public Debt, by Instrument
(In percent of GNP)

Sources: Country authorities and IMF staff estimates.

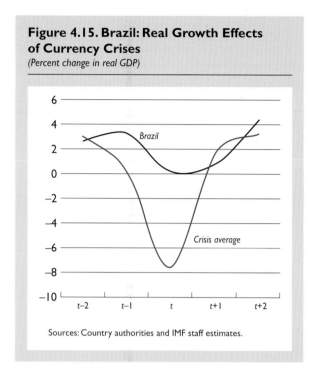

Figure 4.15. Brazil: Real Growth Effects of Currency Crises
(Percent change in real GDP)

Sources: Country authorities and IMF staff estimates.

debt to help banks close their open foreign currency positions. Finally, in an effort to avoid a collapse of the banking system, the government declared a blanket guarantee for banks' liabilities and issued bonds for their recapitalization. As a result, the government's debt from bank recapitalization alone reached almost 30 percent of GNP, contributing to a jump in gross public debt to 86 percent of GNP by the end of 2001.

Brazil: How the Public Sector Leveraged Its Balance Sheet to Insulate the Private Sector from the 1998–99 Currency Crisis

Contrary to other recent currency crises, the Brazilian economy posted positive real growth rates even during the crisis years of 1998 and 1999 (Figure 4.15). Brazil's resilience is particularly remarkable given the large currency and maturity mismatches within the banking and corporate sectors in the run-up to the crisis (Figure 4.16—the vertical dotted lines mark the two major crises during the time period shown). This achievement can be attributed to the authorities' (implicit) decision to address key balance sheet vulnerabilities ahead of the change in exchange rate regime by transferring risks to the government's balance sheet. This section details this strategy in terms of its costs and benefits and how it subsequently changed the vulnerability of Brazil's public sector.

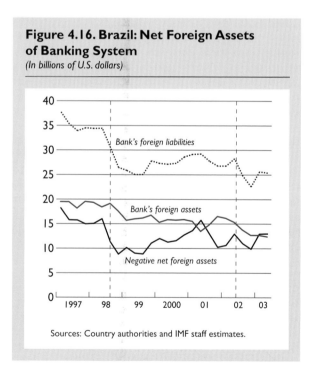

Figure 4.16. Brazil: Net Foreign Assets of Banking System
(In billions of U.S. dollars)

Sources: Country authorities and IMF staff estimates.

A supportive external environment toward emerging markets in the mid-1990s allowed both the financial and corporate sectors to build up large stocks of external debt. These sectors took advantage of the lower nominal interest rates on debt issued externally and the perception that currency risk was limited. Brazil was following a crawling peg exchange rate regime at the time, which had played an important role in successfully bringing down hyperinflation and stabilizing the economy. The private sector's external debt peaked during the fourth quarter of 1998 at US$146 billion (including intercompany loans).

The increase of foreign assets in the banking system did not keep pace with the buildup of foreign liabilities. At the beginning of 1997, the negative net foreign asset position of the banking system was around US$20 billion (excluding holdings of dollar-linked debt, which at the time had reached US$15 billion). In the corporate sector, companies in both the nontradable and tradable sectors were heavy borrowers, increasing their external debt substantially from 1997 onward (Figure 4.17). Within the corporate sector, the utility and telecommunications sectors had the largest currency mismatches.

The market turmoil that started in October 1997 triggered a sharp increase in demand for hedge by both the banking and the corporate sectors. In a rush to close large net open foreign exchange positions, demand for dollar-linked government domestic debt and outright spot purchases of dollars surged; the authorities responded by increasing the stock of dollar-linked debt outstanding by nearly US$20 billion. In 1998 pressure on the exchange rate rapidly intensified, as slippages emerged in fiscal adjustment and the central bank lowered interest rates prematurely, forcing it to intervene once again to support the crawling peg. Market participants used the time provided to them by active central bank intervention in both spot and futures markets, combined with stepped-up issuance of dollar-linked domestic debt, to reduce further their net open foreign exchange positions. Through the issuance of an additional US$23 billion in dollar-linked debt after the end of 1997, mainly to roll over public debt amortizations falling due, and accumulated foreign exchange intervention of US$30 billion, the authorities ensured that the local banking system was actually net long on dollars by the end of 1998.[39] Moreover, most of the corporate sector was by then protected from the devaluation that took place only a few weeks later.

As part of its defense of the exchange rate, the central bank also more than doubled overnight interest rates, exposing the maturity mismatch of the banking system. The overnight rate was hiked from 19 percent at the beginning of September 1998 to more than 40 percent in November. The banking system's maturity mismatch was partly mitigated

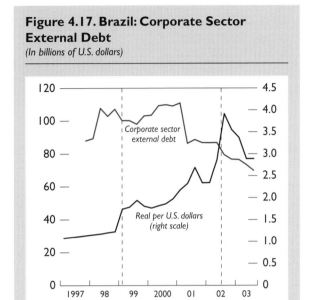

Figure 4.17. Brazil: Corporate Sector External Debt
(In billions of U.S. dollars)

Sources: Country authorities and IMF staff estimates.

by a sharp pickup in sovereign issuance of bonds linked to the overnight interest rate, which allowed the government to partially trade off rollover risk by assuming the banks' interest rate risk. As part of a strategy of stabilizing market sentiment in the aftermath of the float, the overnight rate was once again raised to 45 percent, but at this time the banking system had largely shifted its government debt holdings to overnight-linked instruments and thus stood ready to gain from the move.

As a by-product of the Brazilian authorities' attempt to defend the crawling peg and hence immunize large parts of the banking and corporate sectors, Brazilian banks posted record profits during the first quarter of 1999. This experience differs sharply from other countries' banking systems in the aftermath of exiting a fixed exchange rate regime. As a sign of the corporate sector's ability to weather the storm, the banking sector's nonperforming loans rose only modestly from 7.6 percent of total loans in 1997 to 10.2 percent in 1998, and fell back again to 8.7 percent in 1999.

Far from entering into a recession, the economy actually grew slightly in real terms in 1999. Unaffected by wealth effects, the economy was able to avoid most of the collateral damage from the currency crisis. Confidence was restored, as inflation and inflation expectations were rapidly brought under control by proactive monetary policy. The authorities were also able deliver on a significant fiscal adjustment that alleviated debt sustainability concerns. This fiscal adjustment was based on far-reaching reforms to increase

---

[39]Resulting in a stock of dollar-linked debt of US$56 billion by the end of 1998.

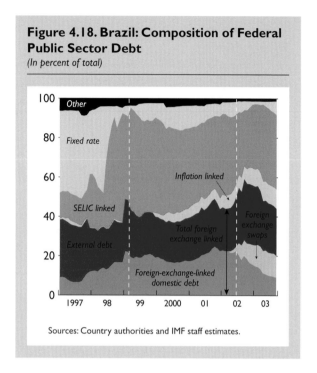

Figure 4.18. Brazil: Composition of Federal Public Sector Debt
(In percent of total)

Sources: Country authorities and IMF staff estimates.

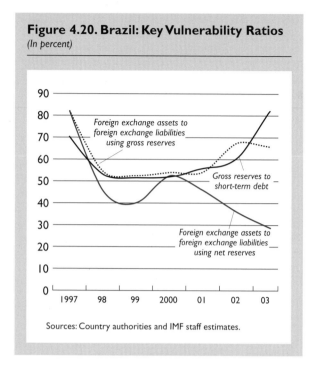

Figure 4.20. Brazil: Key Vulnerability Ratios
(In percent)

Sources: Country authorities and IMF staff estimates.

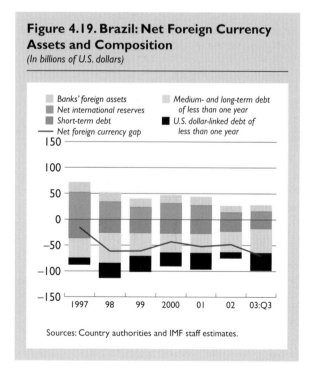

Figure 4.19. Brazil: Net Foreign Currency Assets and Composition
(In billions of U.S. dollars)

Sources: Country authorities and IMF staff estimates.

fiscal discipline at all levels of government. Public indebtedness was further constrained through a system of spending rules, borrowing limits, and sanctions.

The Brazilian government's ability largely to insulate the banking and corporate sectors from a more than 30 percent exchange rate depreciation reflected the strength of its own balance sheet going into the crisis. At the end of December 1997, Brazil's public sector net debt was a relatively modest 35 percent of GDP, and nearly 50 percent of its public debt was held either in short-term fixed rate notes or in inflation-indexed debt. The authorities' response to the currency crisis not only triggered a sharp rise in the net debt to GDP ratio to 53 percent by the end of 1999, but also markedly changed the composition of its debt. The share of dollar-linked domestic debt doubled, while the share of overnight-linked bonds more than tripled to account for more than 50 percent of total public debt by the second quarter of 1999. Coming out of the currency crisis, more than 90 percent of Brazil's public debt was either linked to the exchange rate or the overnight rate, making the debt stock exceedingly vulnerable to future shocks (Figure 4.18).[40]

The shift of the corporate and banking sectors' currency mismatches to the public sector's balance sheet did not significantly reduce the overall economy's exposure to exchange rate changes. As shown in Figure 4.19, the net gap between foreign exchange liabilities and assets of the economy improved only marginally in 1999 and subsequently largely stabilized. Stylized balance sheet indicators comparing the economy's liquid foreign assets to its short-term foreign liabilities

---

[40]In addition to traditional foreign exchange intervention in the spot and futures markets, the government replaced, in essence, the financial and corporate sectors' market risk (risk related to the exchange rate, interest rates, and so on) with credit risk to the government.

(Figure 4.20) imply a worsening in Brazil's external vulnerability following the 1998 crisis. However, most of this reflects the deterioration in the public sector's balance sheet after it assumed a large share of the private sector's maturity and currency mismatches.[41] The corporate and banking sectors, in contrast, gradually reduced their foreign currency exposure and shifted their net financing onshore in the context of a floating exchange rate regime. Moreover, the stock-based metrics in Figure 4.20 does not capture the impressive turnaround in Brazil's current account balance and the economy's increased overall resistance to shocks following the switch to a flexible exchange rate regime.

Peru: How a Highly Dollarized Economy Remained Resilient in the Face of Regional Financial Turmoil

Despite being one of the most highly dollarized economies in Latin America, Peru weathered well the turbulences that adversely affected other dollarized economies in the region at the beginning of this decade. Peru's financial dollarization ranked among the highest in Latin America (measured as a share of dollar deposits in total bank deposits) at the end of 2001: Bolivia (91 percent), Uruguay (85 percent), Peru (74 percent), Argentina (74 percent), and Paraguay (67 percent). Following Argentina's default, most of these countries experienced more or less severe crises, which were closely related to the pervasive currency mismatches that dollarization had created on domestic balance sheets. In contrast, Peru's economy remained stable and even achieved robust growth. A closer look at the composition of the economy's sectoral balance sheets and their linkages (at the end of 2002) may help to explain the country's resilience.

Peru's high domestic liability dollarization is clearly reflected in the large shares of foreign currency debt across sectors at the end of 2002. Over three-fourths of all debt in Peru was denominated in foreign currency (about 100 percent of GDP), but only about half of this was owed to external creditors (Figure 4.21). While the share of foreign currency debt was relatively evenly distributed, the share of external debt varied widely across sectors: highest in the public sector—reflecting the government's dependence on external financing—and very low in the private financial sector.

The resulting currency mismatches differed across sectors—implying that a currency depreciation would affect sectoral balance sheets quite differently (Figure 4.22).

---

[41]Additional vulnerabilities may be generated by the possible moral hazard created by the implicit public guarantee of private foreign currency liabilities.

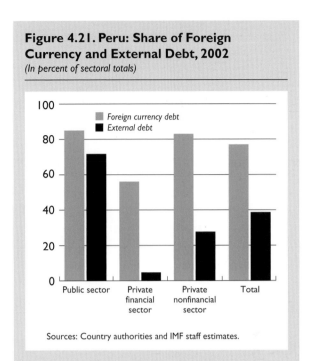

Figure 4.21. Peru: Share of Foreign Currency and External Debt, 2002
(In percent of sectoral totals)

Sources: Country authorities and IMF staff estimates.

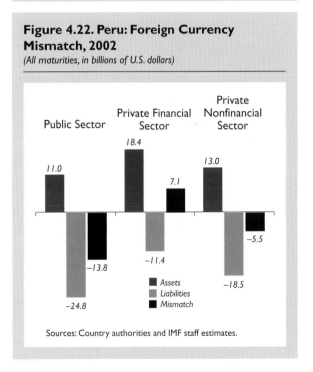

Figure 4.22. Peru: Foreign Currency Mismatch, 2002
(All maturities, in billions of U.S. dollars)

Sources: Country authorities and IMF staff estimates.

• The currency mismatch in the *public sector* was by far the largest. This was mitigated, however, by a favorable maturity structure and a very liquid position vis-à-vis nonresidents, mainly owing to the central bank's large international reserves. The bulk of the public sector's short-term dollar liabilities were domestic (the banking system's dollar

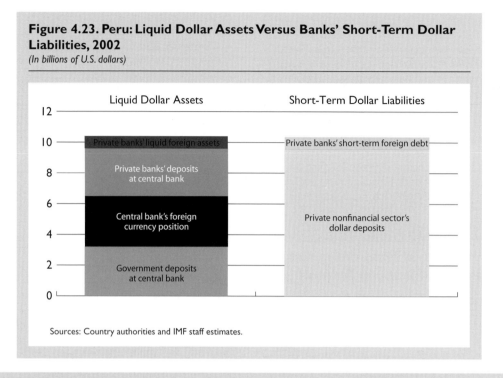

Figure 4.23. Peru: Liquid Dollar Assets Versus Banks' Short-Term Dollar Liabilities, 2002
(In billions of U.S. dollars)

Sources: Country authorities and IMF staff estimates.

Table 4.4. Peru: Foreign Currency Debt and Foreign Currency Income in the Private Nonfinancial Sector[1]
(In billions of U.S. dollars)

	Domestic Loans in U.S. Dollars	External Debt[2]	Exports of Goods and Services	Imported Inputs[3]	Total debt	Net Export Earnings
Manufacturing industry	4.1	0.4	4.6	2.3	3.1	−0.7
Primary sector	1.5	5.6	7.1	5.3	1.5	3.8
Transportation	0.7	0.1	0.7	0.3	0.1	0.2
Commerce	1.8	—	1.8	—	—	0.0
Services	1.3	0.2	1.5	1.0	0.2	0.7
Construction	1.3	—	1.3	—	—	0.0
Other	1.1	0.1	1.1	0.3	0.1	0.2
Total	11.8	6.3	18.1	9.2	5.0	4.2

Sources: Peruvian authorities and IMF staff estimates.

[1]Using the banking system's loan portfolio classification.

[2]Assuming medium- and long-term debt is owed by mining corporations, and allocating trade credit by export weight.

[3]Intermediary goods and certain service imports (transportation, communications, and insurance); weighted by export share where importing sector is unspecified.

deposits at the central bank), and most of its external liabilities were multilateral and bilateral loans with long maturities.

• The *private financial sector's* dollar intermediation created a large maturity mismatch in foreign currency. Banks partly addressed this vulnerability by maintaining a liquidity ratio (liquid assets over short-term liabilities) in foreign currency twice as high as in local currency. Over 90 percent of the financial sector's short-term funding came from residents, who had proven to be a less volatile funding source than external credit lines (Figure 4.23).

• The *private nonfinancial sector's* overall balance between short-term foreign currency assets and liabilities remained positive, although half of the

Figure 4.24. Peru: Liquid Dollar Assets Versus Banks' Dollar Liabilities and Short-Term Foreign Debt, 2002

(In billions of U.S. dollars)

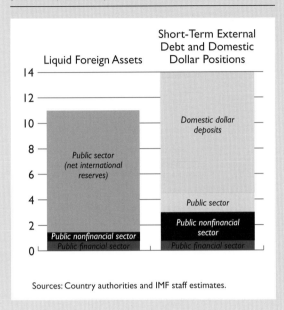

Sources: Country authorities and IMF staff estimates.

of the private nonfinancial sector's dollar deposits in the domestic banking system. This helped to avoid the creation of negative expectations, which could have led to self-fulfilling bank runs. Moreover, high official reserves also mitigated the risk of an external rollover crisis. The private financial sector's liquid external assets almost exactly matched its short-term foreign debt, and the private nonfinancial sector had a favorable mismatch (i.e., assets exceeded liabilities) between liquid foreign assets and short-term external debt. The public sector's reserve holdings were, in principle, high enough to help bridge a temporary loss of access to foreign credit (Figure 4.24).

The composition of Peru's sectoral balance sheets thus made it resilient to anything but the extreme scenario of a simultaneous run on domestic dollar deposits and a shutdown of external credit. The sum of short-term debt and domestic dollar deposits at the end of 2002 exceeded the sum of official reserves and the private sector's liquid foreign assets. This static comparison of assets and liabilities, however, does not take into account a possible flow adjustment in the current account in response to a depreciated exchange rate, which could help to mitigate any gaps caused by a simultaneous run on deposits and shutdown of credit. Moreover, examination of end-2002 data alone misses the fact that high coverage of potential foreign currency needs had been maintained over time (Figure 4.25): Peru's official reserves together with banks' liquid foreign assets consistently covered two-thirds to three-fourths of the sum of the country's short-term

dollar loans from domestic banks had to be rolled over every year. This overall match, however, only resulted from the sector's large dollar deposits with domestic banks. Individual entities or entire subsectors could still have large mismatches if, for example, a large part of deposits were held by households, but most loans were owed by corporations.

Consequently, the financial sector's credit exposure to the private nonfinancial sector was a central transmission channel for possible depreciation-induced balance sheet problems. Over 60 percent of banks' assets at the end of 2002 were dollar loans to the private nonfinancial sector, making their performance under a depreciated exchange rate critical to solvency. In this context, once doubt would rise about the private financial sector's solvency, the risk of a run on dollar deposits would also rise and expose the sector's maturity mismatch. The composition of banks' loan portfolios suggests that a significant share of their dollar loans was extended to industries with little export activity (Table 4.4). Producers of nontradable goods—construction, commerce, and other services—alone made up over a third of the banking system's loan portfolio.

Against this backdrop, the public sector's ability to act as a lender of last resort became crucial for depositors' confidence. The central bank's high official reserve holdings at the end of 2002 matched the stock

Figure 4.25. Peru: External and Financial Vulnerability Ratios

(In percent)

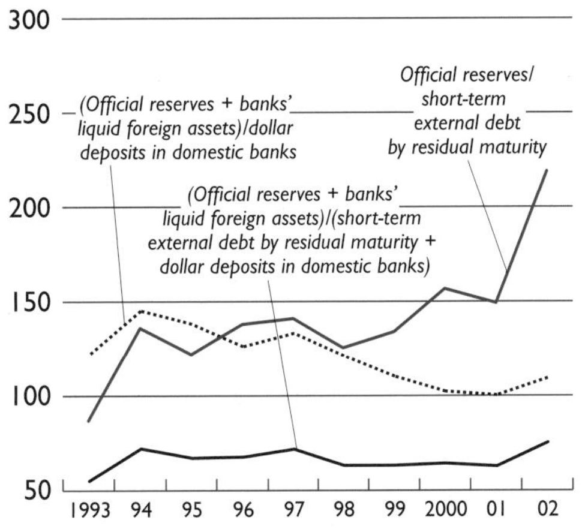

Sources: Country authorities and IMF staff estimates.

external debt and domestic dollar deposits. This significant liquidity buffer is likely to have boosted confidence in critical moments and helped Peru's highly dollarized economy to weather difficult periods, such as that during Brazil's election campaign in 2002.

Lebanon: How Confidence Can Uphold Fragile Balance Sheets

Despite long-time concerns about the sustainability of its public debt, Lebanon has successfully been able to avoid a crisis.[42] The public sector balance sheet has long been the country's key vulnerability: gross public debt (excluding monetary liabilities) at some 180 percent of GDP and gross financing needs of some 45 percent of GDP in 2002 are far beyond the ratios typically seen in emerging market countries. Yet, Lebanon has defied pessimistic predictions, including those of the IMF, and a debt crisis has been avoided. While investor confidence plays a key role in any emerging market economy, the following analysis highlights how in Lebanon it has become the linchpin of a unique symbiosis between the public and the banking sectors' balance sheets. The analysis also shows how investor confidence allowed the authorities to overcome the near-rollover crisis of 2001–02.

The structure of Lebanon's public debt stock magnifies the risks created by its size (Figure 4.26), notably:

- *Exchange rate risk.* The share of foreign-currency-denominated debt is high and has increased in recent years (from only 30 percent in 2000 to 50 percent at the end of 2003), in part because of exceptional donor financing in 2002 (commonly dubbed "Paris II") and higher central bank foreign currency liabilities;

- *Rollover risk.* About the same proportion of debt has a residual maturity of one year or less, although Paris II financing and a domestic debt exchange in early 2002 helped lengthen the average maturity of public debt; and

- *Interest rate risk.* Although the share of floating rate public debt is low, the debt's short average maturity implies that a change in market interest rates would be reflected almost entirely in the servicing costs of domestic currency debt within two years.

The main rollover and interest rate risks of the public sector are borne by the domestic banking sector, which constitutes the public sector's main funding source. Less than 15 percent of the public sec-

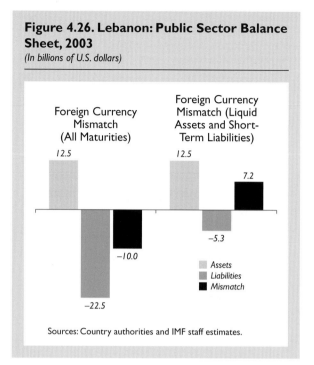

Figure 4.26. Lebanon: Public Sector Balance Sheet, 2003
(In billions of U.S. dollars)

Sources: Country authorities and IMF staff estimates.

tor's debt is owed to nonresidents (who mostly hold foreign currency debt). The remainder of public debt is held by residents, mainly domestic banks. Thus, it is the domestic banking sector's willingness to roll over its public debt holdings—without demanding a much larger risk premium—that determines the sustainability of public debt.

Banks' ability to roll over the public debt, in turn, depends on their ability to renew their own monetary liabilities. The banking sector's impressive deposit base—total deposits, including nonresident deposits, stand at some 275 percent of GDP—has made its financing of the government possible. Any difficulty banks may have in rolling over these deposits (e.g., due to changes in money demand) would be reflected in an interest rate adjustment and/or a liquidation of public sector liabilities by drawing down central bank reserves.

Depositors' confidence, in turn, is closely related to their risk perception about public debt, which is the banking sector's main asset. Banks' claims on the public sector make up about 40 percent of their total assets.[43] Hence, depositors' confidence in the viability of banks' balance sheets, and their confidence in the performance of public debt, are highly interdependent. Interestingly, as detailed below, depositors have been largely unfazed by the rise in public debt.

---

[42]The discussion in this section focuses on the period 2000–04 and does not reflect developments in the wake of Lebanon's political crisis in early 2005.

[43]Including all deposit money banks, but excluding nonbank financial institutions.

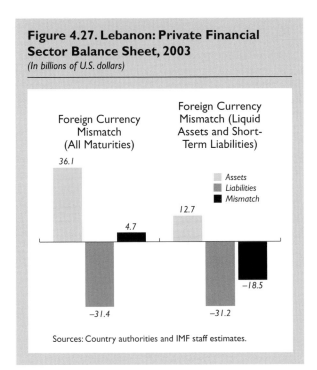

Figure 4.27. Lebanon: Private Financial Sector Balance Sheet, 2003
(In billions of U.S. dollars)

Sources: Country authorities and IMF staff estimates.

At the same time, the dollarization of the banking sector's liability side has created a substantial maturity mismatch in foreign currency (Figure 4.27). The funding of banks is not only very short term (95 percent of liabilities are short-term deposits), but also largely denominated in foreign currency (about 70 percent of total deposits are denominated in U.S. dollars). Although these deposits are mostly from residents (nonresidents account for only 15 percent of the deposits base), the maturity mismatch in foreign currency constitutes a substantial risk.[44] Excluding dollar-denominated lending to the nonbank private sector (which does not represent liquid assets), the banking sector's foreign exchange position is significantly shorter. The limited liquidity coverage of foreign-currency-denominated liabilities is, thus, a key vulnerability in the event of a sizable and rapid withdrawal of such deposits.

Against this background, the public sector's ample—and increasing—reserve holdings have played an important role in building confidence. The recent growth of official reserves (to US$12.5 billion by the end of 2003)—increasing at a faster pace than the central bank's foreign currency liabilities—has contributed to a boost in confidence in three ways. First, in the absence of any regular dollar revenues, the holdings of foreign currency assets are critical to gauge the foreign currency mismatch on the public sector balance sheet: although the overall mismatch

remains substantial, liquid assets comfortably exceed liabilities falling due over the short term. Second, higher official reserves also signal an increase in emergency liquidity that could be made available to back some (though certainly not all) dollar deposits in the banking system. Finally, high reserves are widely seen as a guarantor of the exchange rate peg, which is perceived as essential to economic and social stability. Aware of its crucial signaling function, the central bank has taken an active stance toward accumulating reserves, by, inter alia, issuing certificates of deposit at relatively high yields.[45] The authorities deem the benefits of such operations as great enough to justify their substantial quasi-fiscal costs.

Lately, improved risk perception has created a virtuous circle of growing reserves, higher money demand and falling spreads on government debt. The increase in official reserves after Paris II was accompanied by a surge in investors' confidence, against the background of a favorable interest rate environment and sizable capital inflows from countries in the Middle East. This increased confidence led to strong growth in total deposits (reaching 15 percent in 2003) and a sharp decline in the sovereign risk premium.[46] The resulting liquidity relief provided the banking sector with ample resources that it could recycle to fund the public sector, and which, in turn, was able to place its debt at lower interest cost.

This circular effect, however, can also work in the opposite direction, as evidenced in the near-crisis episode of 2001–02. Developments in the run-up to the Paris II donor conference in late 2002 give an indication of how the cycle's mechanics can also turn vicious. When official reserves fell and the growth of money demand slowed down, banks had difficulties increasing their monetary liabilities. Consequently, they tried to reduce their exposure to government paper—by not rolling it over or by discounting it at the central bank—and the subsequent lack of liquidity put upward pressure on interest rates. The central bank had to finance the government directly with an offsetting further loss of foreign reserves. This negative spiral was reversed in mid-2002, when the authorities were able to generate a series of good news to boost investors' confidence. This included initial success with an ambitious fiscal adjustment program, a political truce between the president and prime minister over privatization plans, a surge of reported reserves through a large sale of Eurobonds

[44]By and large, Lebanese expatriates are considered residents.

[45]While denominated in domestic currency, banks could only purchase these CDs by surrendering an equivalent amount of foreign exchange.

[46]Besides growing official reserves, other factors, such as the expected direction of fiscal policy, also played a role in the sovereign risk rating.

to a friendly government, and announcements about the imminent Paris II donor conference.

More fundamentally, some factors idiosyncratic to Lebanon may explain the remarkable resilience of its banking system. The continuous funding of very high public financing needs through the domestic banking system is made possible by a large and dedicated investor base (i.e., the Lebanese diaspora and Arab investors). Indeed, indications are that inflows from regional investors have increased as a result of events post-September 11 (driven by fear that assets held in the United States could be frozen). The government's ability to mobilize extraordinary levels of official financing (such as Paris II) may also play a role.

V Conclusions

This occasional paper illustrates how sectoral balance sheet relationships have evolved over time and how this matters for vulnerability analysis in emerging markets. By several measures, the external, public, nonfinancial, and financial sectors have grown more integrated over the past decade, with the latter playing a particularly important role in channeling and amplifying risks. As the case studies show, these transmission mechanisms bear both risks and opportunities at times of financial crisis. If poorly managed, sectoral balance sheet mismatches can reinforce each other and quickly snowball into the full-blown balance of payments crises witnessed in Argentina, Turkey, or Uruguay. But if the authorities are aware of vulnerabilities and are willing to act, they can preempt or mitigate external shocks, by strengthening confidence (as in Lebanon) or shifting risks from weaker to stronger sectors (as in Brazil and Peru). In practice, emerging market governments have often drawn on their own balance sheet—in the first instance their official reserves, and in the second instance their ability to raise taxes or tap foreign credit lines (including from the IMF). If the public sector is perceived to be taking responsibility for private sector mismatches, such implicit bailout guarantees raise questions of moral hazard.

This paper provides some empirical backing for the need for sound liquidity management as a primary tool for crisis prevention. Specifically, the analysis: (1) underscores the importance of temporary asset buffers associated with strong public sector balance sheets (as well as flexible exchange rates) to limit immediate disruptions and give time to implement appropriate policy responses; (2) highlights the benefits of promoting appropriate buffers and hedges in private balance sheets, which would improve risk allocation within and between sectors; (3) supports the strengthening of banking supervision to limit currency exposure (including to borrowers without foreign currency earnings) and maturity mismatches; and (4) shows how sound liability management by both the public and private sectors can play a major role in containing interest rate, currency, and rollover risk.

At the operational level, the paper shows that existing data sources can go some way to allow for intersectoral balance sheet analysis. Both the cross-country comparison in Section III and the case studies in Section IV rely on data readily available from public sources (such as the IMF's *International Financial Statistics*, World Bank, and BIS databases) or, in some cases, obtained by country teams from their national counterparts. While recent statistical initiatives (SDDS and the IMF's coordinated Portfolio Investment Survey) have contributed to improved balance sheet data, large information gaps exist. Sometimes, however, these can be overcome by making pragmatic assumptions (e.g., that banks maintain no open foreign currency positions, if this is required by supervisory regulations). In balance sheet analysis, the perfect can be the enemy of the good: not all questions require a full intersectoral asset-liability matrix as presented in Box 2.1 above. This is not to deny, however, that more systematic data gathering across the membership would greatly improve the quality of analysis.

An initial step toward operationalizing the BSA would be to complete the analysis for "low-hanging fruit"—simple ratios that can be easily calculated and compared across countries and time. Comprehensive indices of currency and maturity mismatches have recently been proposed, inter alia, by Goldstein and Turner (2003) and the M*f*Risk model. Rather than one single indicator, the present paper uses a range of ratios to gauge various balance sheet risks, which are summarized in the diamond presentation in Figures 3.20 to 3.22 in Section III. Such intertemporal and interregional comparisons provide a natural calibration of the ratios, with the caveats noted above. For example, a first assessment of a member country's vulnerabilities could be obtained by mapping a set of national mismatch indicators against regional comparators. A multidimensional and flexible use of a variety of indicators also responds to concerns regarding a "one-size-fits-all" or mechanistic approach to vulnerability analysis.

Further analytical and empirical work is under way in the IMF to utilize the balance sheet approach for vulnerability analysis (Box 5.1). The examples pre-

---

Box 5.1. Extensions of the Balance Sheet Approach in the IMF

The basic accounting exercise presented in this paper is being refined and extended throughout the IMF, especially with respect to the corporate sector. Initiatives to further operationalize the approach include the following:

A *"bottom-up" compilation of corporate data.* Some of the IMF's vulnerability analysis, especially in Asian countries, draws on detailed studies of corporate data, based on the commercially available Worldscope database. Unlike the macroeconomic approach used in this paper, indicators are derived from firm-level information and aggregated across subsectors. However, many difficulties remain to be resolved, such as differing accounting standards and valuation problems.

Improving comparability across sectors and countries. Excel add-in components are now available that provide easy access to a variety of corporate risk indicators in comparable industries and countries. Measures of risk are derived from the above-mentioned Worldscope database.

Applying the contingent claims approach. This methodology allows one to estimate the risks of default

and the associated value of a risk transfer across the interrelated balance sheets of the corporate, financial, and public sectors (Gapen, Gray, Lim, and Xiao, 2004). For this purpose a commercially available simulation model, Moody's MfRisk, is being applied by rating agencies and the IMF to several countries (e.g., Brazil and Thailand). However, the model is a "black box," which makes the results not always easy to interpret.

Integrating the BSA into early warning systems. A paper by Mulder, Perrelli, and Rocha (2002) finds that the BSA can enhance modern early warning models. Using commercial data for individual corporations in about 20 emerging market countries, the authors find that a number of corporate balance sheet indicators have a measurable relationship to the likelihood of a financial crisis. These include such measures as: (1) the ratio of debt to equity; (2) the ratio of short-term debt to working capital; (3) the corporate share of bank loans times the debt-equity ratio; and (4) the ratio of private sector external debt to exports. Nevertheless, in early warning systems balance sheet indicators can only supplement, rather than substitute for, traditional macroeconomic variables.

---

sented in this paper are a first tentative step—necessarily impeded by the paucity of data—in a wider effort to use balance sheet analysis in bilateral and multilateral surveillance. In parallel, the BSA is being employed in an increasing number of Article IV consultations. The BSA's input to policy dialogue and advice should point to areas in which the approach can be further refined. As better statistical information becomes available, the scope of both the indicators and the member countries covered in cross-country analysis can be expanded. In addition, one could seek further insights into balance sheet vulnerabilities by incorporating off-balance-sheet transactions into the analysis, and by using a more disaggregated sectoral breakdown—even if data limitations necessitate reliance on a smaller sample of countries. Moreover, the BSA could be extended to take into account the main channels of financial contagion identified in the literature. Another promising avenue of further

work is the application of the contingent claims approach, which extends the static balance sheets compiled along the lines described in this paper to a stress-testing analysis.

In its surveillance, the IMF is striving to apply the BSA to its entire membership, where appropriate. The obvious currency and maturity mismatches in emerging market countries have dictated the early focus on these countries, including in this occasional paper. A closer look at industrial countries (and their differences from emerging markets) could yield important insights. Indeed, balance sheet vulnerabilities relevant to mature markets, such as unfunded pension liabilities or asset price bubbles, are steadily moving to center stage in the IMF's Article IV consultations with these countries. While a useful tool, the BSA is far from becoming a standard or even prescribed element of IMF surveillance.

References

Aghion, Philippe, Philippe Bacchetta, and Abhijit Banerjee, 2000, "A Simple Model of Monetary Policy and Currency Crises," *European Economic Review*, Vol. 44 (May), pp. 728–38.

———, 2001a, "Currency Crises and Monetary Policy in an Economy with Credit Constraints," *European Economic Review*, Vol. 45 (June), pp. 1121–50.

———, 2001b, "A Corporate Balance Sheet Approach to Currency Crises," Discussion Paper No. 3092 (London: Centre for Economic Policy Research).

Allen, Mark, Christoph B. Rosenberg, Christian Keller, Brad Setser, and Nouriel Roubini, 2002, "A Balance Sheet Approach to Financial Crisis," IMF Working Paper No. 02/210 (Washington: International Monetary Fund).

Baliño, Tomás J.T., Adam Bennett, and Eduardo Borensztein, 1999, *Monetary Policy in Dollarized Economies*, IMF Occasional Paper No. 171 (Washington: International Monetary Fund).

Borensztein, Eduardo, and Paolo Mauro, 2002, "Reviving the Case for GDP-Indexed Bonds," IMF Policy Discussion Paper No. 02/10 (Washington: International Monetary Fund).

Borensztein, Eduardo, Marcos Chamon, Olivier Jeanne, Paulo Mauro, and Jeromin Zettelmeyer, 2004, *Sovereign Debt Structure for Crisis Prevention*, IMF Occasional Paper No. 237 (Washington: International Monetary Fund).

Burnside, Craig, Martin Eichenbaum, and Sergio Rebelo, 1998, "Prospective Deficits and the Asian Currency Crisis," NBER Working Paper No. 6758 (Cambridge, Massachusetts: National Bureau of Economic Research).

Bussière, Matthieu, and Christian Mulder, 1999, "External Vulnerability in Emerging Market Economies: How High Liquidity Can Offset Weak Fundamentals and the Effects of Contagion," IMF Working Paper No. 99/88 (Washington: International Monetary Fund).

Caballero, Ricardo J., and Arvind Krishnamurthy, 2000, "Dollarization of Liabilities: Underinsurance and Domestic Financial Underdevelopment," NBER Working Paper No. 7792 (Cambridge, Massachusetts: National Bureau of Economic Research).

Calvo, Guillermo, 1998, "Capital Flows and Capital-Market Crises: The Simple Economics of Sudden Stops," *Journal of Applied Economics*, Vol. 1 (November), pp. 35–54.

Calvo, Guillermo, and Carmen M. Reinhart, 2000, "When Capital Inflows Suddenly Stop: Consequences and Policy Options," in *Reforming the International Monetary and Financial System*, ed. by Peter B. Kenen and Alexander K. Swoboda (Washington: International Monetary Fund).

———, 2002, "Fear of Floating," *Quarterly Journal of Economics*, Vol. 117, No. 2 (May), pp. 379–408.

Calvo, Guillermo, Alejandro Izquierdo, and Luis-Fernando Mejía, 2004, "On the Empirics of Sudden Stops: The Relevance of Balance-Sheet Effects," NBER Working Paper No. 10520 (Cambridge, Massachusetts: National Bureau of Economic Research).

Cavallo, Michele, Kate Kisselev, Fabrizio Perri, and Nouriel Roubini, 2002, "Exchange Rate Overshooting and the Costs of Floating" (unpublished; New York: New York University).

Céspedes, Luis Felipe, Roberto Chang, and Andrés Velasco, 2000, "Balance Sheets and Exchange Rate Policy," NBER Working Paper No. 7840 (Cambridge, Massachusetts: National Bureau of Economic Research).

Chang, Roberto, and Andrés Velasco, 1999, "Liquidity Crises in Emerging Markets: Theory and Policy," NBER Working Paper No. 7272 (Cambridge, Massachusetts: National Bureau of Economic Research).

Cole, Harold L., and Patrick J. Kehoe, 1996, "A Self-Fulfilling Model of Mexico's 1994–1995 Debt Crisis," *Journal of International Economics*, Vol. 41 (November), pp. 309–30.

Collyns, Charles, and G. Russell Kincaid, eds., 2003, *Managing Financial Crises: Recent Experience and Lessons for Latin America*, IMF Occasional Paper No. 217 (Washington: International Monetary Fund).

Corsetti, Giancarlo, Paolo Pesenti, and Nouriel Roubini, 1999a, "What Caused the Asian Currency and Financial Crisis?" *Japan and the World Economy*, Vol. 11 (October), pp. 305–73.

———, 1999b, "Paper Tigers? A Model of the Asian Crisis," *European Economic Review*, Vol. 43 (June), pp. 1211–36.

Corsetti, Giancarlo, Amil Dasgupta, Stephen Morris, and Hyun Song Shin, 2004, "Does One Soros Make a Difference? A Theory of Currency Crises with Large and Small Traders," *Review of Economic Studies*, Vol. 71 (January), pp. 87–113.

Daseking, Christina, Atish Ghosh, Timothy Lane, and Alun Thomas, 2004, *Lessons from the Crisis in Argentina*, IMF Occasional Paper No. 236 (Washington: International Monetary Fund).

De Nicoló, Gianni, Patrick Honohan, and Alain Ize, 2003, "Dollarization of the Banking System: Good or Bad?" IMF Working Paper No. 03/146 (Washington: International Monetary Fund).

Diamond, Douglas, and Philip Dybvig, 1983, "Bank Runs, Deposit Insurance, and Liquidity," *Journal of Political Economy*, Vol. 91 (June), pp. 401–19.

Diamond, Douglas W., and Raghuram G. Rajan, 2000, "Banks, Short Term Debt and Financial Crises: Theory, Policy Implications and Applications," NBER Working Paper No. 7764 (Cambridge, Massachusetts: National Bureau of Economic Research).

Drazen, Allan, and Paul R. Masson, 1994, "Credibility of Policies Versus Credibility of Policymakers," *Quarterly Journal of Economics*, Vol. 109 (August), pp. 735–54.

Dornbusch, Rudiger, 2001, "A Primer on Emerging Market Crises," NBER Working Paper No. 8326 (Cambridge, Massachusetts: National Bureau of Economic Research).

Edwards, Sebastian, 2001, "Dollarization: Myths and Realities," *Journal of Policy Modeling*, Vol. 23 (April), pp. 249–65.

Eichengreen, Barry, Ricardo Hausmann, and Ugo Panizza, 2003, "Currency Mismatches, Debt Intolerance and Original Sin: Why They Are Not the Same and Why It Matters," NBER Working Paper No. 10036 (Cambridge, Massachusetts: National Bureau of Economic Research).

Flood, Robert P., and Peter M. Garber, 1984, "Collapsing Exchange-Rate Regimes: Some Linear Examples," *Journal of International Economics*, Vol. 17 (August), pp. 1–13.

Gapen, Michael T., Dale F. Gray, Cheng Hoon Lim, and Yingbin Xiao, 2004, "The Contingent Claims Approach to Corporate Vulnerability Analysis: Estimating Default Risk and Economy-Wide Risk Transfer," IMF Working Paper No. 04/121 (Washington: International Monetary Fund).

Garcia, Marcio, and Roberto Rigobon, 2004, "A Risk Management Approach to Emerging Market's Sovereign Debt Sustainability with an Application to Brazilian Data," NBER Working Paper No. 10336 (Cambridge, Massachusetts: National Bureau of Economic Research).

Gertler, Mark, Simon Gilchrist, and Fabio Natalucci, 2003, "External Constraints on Monetary Policy and the Financial Accelerator," NBER Working Paper No. 10128 (Cambridge, Massachusetts: National Bureau of Economic Research).

Goldstein, Morris, and Philip Turner, 2004, *Controlling Currency Mismatches in Emerging Markets* (Washington: Institute for International Economics).

Gulde, Anne-Marie, David Hoelscher, Alain Ize, Alfredo Leone, David Marston, and Marina Moretti, 2003, "Dealing with Banking Crises in Dollarized Economies," in *Managing Financial Crises: Recent Experience and Lessons from Latin America*, ed. by Charles Collyns and G. Russell Kincaid, IMF Occasional Paper No. 217 (Washington: International Monetary Fund).

Hagan, Sean, Eliot Kalter, and Rhoda Weeks-Brown, 2003, "Corporate Debt Restructuring in the Wake of Economic Crisis," in *Managing Financial Crises: Recent Experience and Lessons from Latin America*, ed. by Charles Collyns and G. Russell Kincaid, IMF Occasional Paper No. 217 (Washington: International Monetary Fund).

Havrylyshyn, Oleh, and Christian Beddies, 2003, "Dollarization in the Former Soviet Union: From Hysteria to Hysteresis," *Contemporary Economic Studies*, Vol. 45, No. 3, pp. 329–57.

International Monetary Fund, 1993, *Balance of Payments Manual*, 5th ed. (Washington).

———, 2002a, "Data Provision to the Fund for Surveillance Purposes," available at www.imf.org/external/np/sta/data/prov/2002/042602.htm.

———, 2002b, "Assessing Sustainability," available at www.imf.org/external/np/pdr/sus/2002/eng/052802.htm.

———, 2003a, *World Economic Outlook*, September, World Economic and Financial Surveys (Washington).

———, 2003b, *External Debt Statistics: Guide for Compilers and Users* (Washington).

———, 2003c, "Slovak Republic: 2003 Article IV Consultation—Staff Report, Public Information Notice on the Executive Board Discussion; and Statement by the Executive Director for the Slovak Republic," IMF Country Report No. 03/234 (Washington).

Jeanne, Olivier, and Charles Wyplosz, 2001, "The International Lender of Last Resort: How Large Is Large Enough?" NBER Working Paper No. 8381 (Cambridge, Massachusetts: National Bureau of Economic Research).

J.P. Morgan, 2002, *Guide to Local Markets* (New York).

Kaminsky, Graciela, and Carmen Reinhart, 1999, "The Twin Crises: The Causes of Banking and Balance-of-Payments Problems," *American Economic Review*, Vol. 89 (June), pp. 473–500.

Kester, Anne Y., 2001, *International Reserves and Foreign Currency Liquidity: Guidelines for a Data Template*" (Washington: International Monetary Fund).

Krugman, Paul, 1979, "A Model of Balance-of-Payments Crises," *Journal of Money, Credit and Banking*, Vol. 11, No. 3 (August), pp. 311–25.

———, 1998, "Curfews on Capital Flight: What Are the Options?" available at http://web.mit.edu/krugman/www/curfews.html.

———, 1999, "Balance Sheets, the Transfer Problem, and Financial Crises," in *International Finance and Financial Crises: Essays in Honor of Robert P. Flood, Jr.*, ed. by Peter Isard, Assaf Razin, and Andrew K. Rose (Boston: Kluwer Academic; Washington: International Monetary Fund).

Lagos, Martin, 2002, "The Argentine Banking Crisis 2001–2002," Report prepared for the Argentine Bankers Association.

Lindgren, Carl-Johan, Tomás J.T. Baliño, Charles Enoch, Anne-Marie Gulde, Marc Quintyn, and Leslie Teo, 1999, *Financial Sector Crisis and Restructuring—Lessons from Asia*, IMF Occasional Paper No. 188 (Washington: International Monetary Fund).

Manasse, Paolo, Nouriel Roubini, and Axel Schimmelpfennig, 2003, "Predicting Sovereign Debt Crises," IMF Working Paper No. 03/221 (Washington: International Monetary Fund).

Masson, Paul R., 1999, "Multiple Equilibria, Contagion, and the Emerging Market Crises," IMF Working Paper No. 99/164 (Washington: International Monetary Fund).

Mongardini, Joannes, and Johannes Mueller, 2000, "Ratchet Effects in Currency Substitution: An Application to the Kyrgyz Republic," *IMF Staff Papers*, Vol. 47, No. 2 (December), pp. 218–37.

Morris, Stephen, and Hyun Song Shin, 2003, "Global Games: Theory and Applications," in *Advances in Economics and Econometrics: Theory and Applications, Eighth World Congress, Vol. 1.*, ed. by Mathias Dewatripont, Lars Peter Hansen, and Stephen Turnovsky (Cambridge, England: Cambridge University Press).

Mulder, Christian B., Roberto Perrelli, and Manuel Rocha, 2002, "The Role of Corporate, Legal and Macroeconomic Balance Sheet Indicators in Crisis Detection and Prevention," IMF Working Paper No. 02/59 (Washington: International Monetary Fund).

Obstfeld, Maurice, 1994, "The Logic of Currency Crises," *Cahiers Économiques et Monétaires* (Bank of France), Vol. 43, pp. 189–213.

Oomes, Nienke, 2003, "Network Externalities and Dollarization Hysteresis: The Case of Russia," IMF Working Paper No. 03/96 (Washington: International Monetary Fund).

Pettis, Michael, 2001, *The Volatility Machine: Emerging Economies and the Threat of Their Financial Collapse* (New York: Oxford University Press).

Reinhart, Carmen M., Kenneth S. Rogoff, and Miguel A. Savastano, 2003a, "Debt Intolerance," *Brookings Papers on Economic Activity: 1* (Brookings Institution), pp. 1–74.

———, 2003b, "Addicted to Dollars," NBER Working Paper No. 10015 (Cambridge, Massachusetts: National Bureau of Economic Research).

Rodrik, Dani, and Andrés Velasco, 1999, "Short-Term Capital Flows," NBER Working Paper No. 7364 (Cambridge, Massachusetts: National Bureau of Economic Research).

Roubini, Nouriel, 2001, "Should Argentina Dollarize or Float? The Pros and Cons of Alternative Exchange Rate Regimes and their Implications for Domestic and Foreign Debt Restructuring Reduction" (unpublished; New York: Stern School of Business, New York University).

Sachs, Jeffrey, and Steven Radelet, 1998, "The Onset of the East Asian Financial Crisis," NBER Working Paper No. 6680 (Cambridge, Massachusetts: National Bureau of Economic Research).

Schneider, Martin, and Aaron Tornell, 2000, "Balance Sheet Effects, Bailout Guarantees and Financial Crises," NBER Working Paper No. 8060 (Cambridge, Massachusetts: National Bureau of Economic Research).

Zettelmeyer, Jeromin, and Olivier D. Jeanne, 2002, "'Original Sin,' Balance Sheet Crises, and the Roles of International Lending," IMF Working Paper No. 02/234 (Washington: International Monetary Fund).

Recent Occasional Papers of the International Monetary Fund

240. Debt-Related Vulnerabilities and Financial Crises: An Application of the Balance Sheet Approach to Emerging Market Countries, by Christoph Rosenberg, Ioannis Halikias, Brett House, Christian Keller, Jens Nystedt, Alexander Pitt, and Brad Setser. 2005.

239. GEM: A New International Macroeconomic Model, by Tamim Bayoumi, with assistance from Douglas Laxton, Hamid Faruqee, Benjamin Hunt, Philippe Karam, Jaewoo Lee, Alessandro Rebucci, and Ivan Tchakarov. 2004.

238. Stabilization and Reforms in Latin America: A Macroeconomic Perspective on the Experience Since the Early 1990s, by Anoop Singh, Agnès Belaisch, Charles Collyns, Paula De Masi, Reva Krieger, Guy Meredith, and Robert Rennhack. 2005.

237. Sovereign Debt Structure for Crisis Prevention, by Eduardo Borensztein, Marcos Chamon, Olivier Jeanne, Paolo Mauro, and Jeromin Zettelmeyer. 2004.

236. Lessons from the Crisis in Argentina, by Christina Daseking, Atish R. Ghosh, Alun Thomas, and Timothy Lane. 2004.

235. A New Look at Exchange Rate Volatility and Trade Flows, by Peter B. Clark, Natalia Tamirisa, and Shang-Jin Wei, with Azim Sadikov and Li Zeng. 2004.

234. Adopting the Euro in Central Europe: Challenges of the Next Step in European Integration, by Susan M. Schadler, Paulo F. Drummond, Louis Kuijs, Zuzana Murgasova, and Rachel N. van Elkan. 2004.

233. Germany's Three-Pillar Banking System: Cross-Country Perspectives in Europe, by Allan Brunner, Jörg Decressin, Daniel Hardy, and Beata Kudela. 2004.

232. China's Growth and Integration into the World Economy: Prospects and Challenges, edited by Eswar Prasad. 2004.

231. Chile: Policies and Institutions Underpinning Stability and Growth, by Eliot Kalter, Steven Phillips, Marco A. Espinosa-Vega, Rodolfo Luzio, Mauricio Villafuerte, and Manmohan Singh. 2004.

230. Financial Stability in Dollarized Countries, by Anne-Marie Gulde, David Hoelscher, Alain Ize, David Marston, and Gianni De Nicoló. 2004.

229. Evolution and Performance of Exchange Rate Regimes, by Kenneth S. Rogoff, Aasim M. Husain, Ashoka Mody, Robin Brooks, and Nienke Oomes. 2004.

228. Capital Markets and Financial Intermediation in The Baltics, by Alfred Schipke, Christian Beddies, Susan M. George, and Niamh Sheridan. 2004.

227. U.S. Fiscal Policies and Priorities for Long-Run Sustainability, edited by Martin Mühleisen and Christopher Towe. 2004.

226. Hong Kong SAR: Meeting the Challenges of Integration with the Mainland, edited by Eswar Prasad, with contributions from Jorge Chan-Lau, Dora Iakova, William Lee, Hong Liang, Ida Liu, Papa N'Diaye, and Tao Wang. 2004.

225. Rules-Based Fiscal Policy in France, Germany, Italy, and Spain, by Teresa Dában, Enrica Detragiache, Gabriel di Bella, Gian Maria Milesi-Ferretti, and Steven Symansky. 2003.

224. Managing Systemic Banking Crises, by a staff team led by David S. Hoelscher and Marc Quintyn. 2003.

223. Monetary Union Among Member Countries of the Gulf Cooperation Council, by a staff team led by Ugo Fasano. 2003.

222. Informal Funds Transfer Systems: An Analysis of the Informal Hawala System, by Mohammed El Qorchi, Samuel Munzele Maimbo, and John F. Wilson. 2003.

221. Deflation: Determinants, Risks, and Policy Options, by Manmohan S. Kumar. 2003.

220. Effects of Financial Globalization on Developing Countries: Some Empirical Evidence, by Eswar S. Prasad, Kenneth Rogoff, Shang-Jin Wei, and Ayhan Kose. 2003.

219. Economic Policy in a Highly Dollarized Economy: The Case of Cambodia, by Mario de Zamaroczy and Sopanha Sa. 2003.

218. Fiscal Vulnerability and Financial Crises in Emerging Market Economies, by Richard Hemming, Michael Kell, and Axel Schimmelpfennig. 2003.

217. Managing Financial Crises: Recent Experience and Lessons for Latin America, edited by Charles Collyns and G. Russell Kincaid. 2003.

216. Is the PRGF Living Up to Expectations?—An Assessment of Program Design, by Sanjeev Gupta, Mark Plant, Benedict Clements, Thomas Dorsey, Emanuele Baldacci, Gabriela Inchauste, Shamsuddin Tareq, and Nita Thacker. 2002.

215. Improving Large Taxpayers' Compliance: A Review of Country Experience, by Katherine Baer. 2002.

214. Advanced Country Experiences with Capital Account Liberalization, by Age Bakker and Bryan Chapple. 2002.

213. The Baltic Countries: Medium-Term Fiscal Issues Related to EU and NATO Accession, by Johannes Mueller, Christian Beddies, Robert Burgess, Vitali Kramarenko, and Joannes Mongardini. 2002.

212. Financial Soundness Indicators: Analytical Aspects and Country Practices, by V. Sundararajan, Charles Enoch, Armida San José, Paul Hilbers, Russell Krueger, Marina Moretti, and Graham Slack. 2002.

211. Capital Account Liberalization and Financial Sector Stability, by a staff team led by Shogo Ishii and Karl Habermeier. 2002.

210. IMF-Supported Programs in Capital Account Crises, by Atish Ghosh, Timothy Lane, Marianne Schulze-Ghattas, Aleš Bulíř, Javier Hamann, and Alex Mourmouras. 2002.

209. Methodology for Current Account and Exchange Rate Assessments, by Peter Isard, Hamid Faruqee, G. Russell Kincaid, and Martin Fetherston. 2001.

208. Yemen in the 1990s: From Unification to Economic Reform, by Klaus Enders, Sherwyn Williams, Nada Choueiri, Yuri Sobolev, and Jan Walliser. 2001.

207. Malaysia: From Crisis to Recovery, by Kanitta Meesook, Il Houng Lee, Olin Liu, Yougesh Khatri, Natalia Tamirisa, Michael Moore, and Mark H. Krysl. 2001.

206. The Dominican Republic: Stabilization, Structural Reform, and Economic Growth, by a staff team led by Philip Young comprising Alessandro Giustiniani, Werner C. Keller, and Randa E. Sab and others. 2001.

205. Stabilization and Savings Funds for Nonrenewable Resources, by Jeffrey Davis, Rolando Ossowski, James Daniel, and Steven Barnett. 2001.

204. Monetary Union in West Africa (ECOWAS): Is It Desirable and How Could It Be Achieved? by Paul Masson and Catherine Pattillo. 2001.

203. Modern Banking and OTC Derivatives Markets: The Transformation of Global Finance and Its Implications for Systemic Risk, by Garry J. Schinasi, R. Sean Craig, Burkhard Drees, and Charles Kramer. 2000.

202. Adopting Inflation Targeting: Practical Issues for Emerging Market Countries, by Andrea Schaechter, Mark R. Stone, and Mark Zelmer. 2000.

201. Developments and Challenges in the Caribbean Region, by Samuel Itam, Simon Cueva, Erik Lundback, Janet Stotsky, and Stephen Tokarick. 2000.

200. Pension Reform in the Baltics: Issues and Prospects, by Jerald Schiff, Niko Hobdari, Axel Schimmelpfennig, and Roman Zytek. 2000.

199. Ghana: Economic Development in a Democratic Environment, by Sérgio Pereira Leite, Anthony Pellechio, Luisa Zanforlin, Girma Begashaw, Stefania Fabrizio, and Joachim Harnack. 2000.

198. Setting Up Treasuries in the Baltics, Russia, and Other Countries of the Former Soviet Union: An Assessment of IMF Technical Assistance, by Barry H. Potter and Jack Diamond. 2000.

197. Deposit Insurance: Actual and Good Practices, by Gillian G.H. Garcia. 2000.

196. Trade and Trade Policies in Eastern and Southern Africa, by a staff team led by Arvind Subramanian, with Enrique Gelbard, Richard Harmsen, Katrin Elborgh-Woytek, and Piroska Nagy. 2000.

195. The Eastern Caribbean Currency Union—Institutions, Performance, and Policy Issues, by Frits van Beek, José Roberto Rosales, Mayra Zermeño, Ruby Randall, and Jorge Shepherd. 2000.

194. Fiscal and Macroeconomic Impact of Privatization, by Jeffrey Davis, Rolando Ossowski, Thomas Richardson, and Steven Barnett. 2000.

Note: For information on the titles and availability of Occasional Papers not listed, please consult the IMF's *Publications Catalog* or contact IMF Publication Services.